1

FOCUS

ON

GRAMMAR

AN INTEGRATED SKILLS APPROACH

SECOND EDITION

SAMUELA ECKSTUT

(REVISED BY STACEY HUNTER)

PEARSON

Longman

FOCUS ON GRAMMAR 1: An Integrated Skills Approach
Workbook

Pearson Education, 10 Bank Street, White Plains, NY 10606

Staff credits: The people who made up the *Focus on Grammar 1 Workbook* team, representing
  editorial, production, design, and manufacturing, are: Rhea Banker, Aerin Csigay, Christine
  Edmonds, Nancy Flaggman, Ann France, Laura Le Dréan, Laurie Neaman, Mindy DePalma,
  and Mykan White.
Cover images: background: Comstock Images; background shell and center shell: Nick Koudis
Text composition: ElectraGraphics, Inc.
Text font: 11/13 Sabon, 10/13 Myriad Roman
Illustrators: Steve Attoe, pp. 1 (#1, 2, 3, 4, 6), 2, 5, 6, 8 (a, b, c, d, f, h), 14 (#4), 15, 20, 25, 34, 35, 36,
  41, 46, 47, 51, 52, 56, 61, 66, 68, 70, 72, 74, 75, 78, 79, 82, 86, 87, 91, 92, 104, 105, 106, 109,
  110, 114, 120, 121, 125, 133, 137, 138, 142, 147, 151, 152, 155, 156; Paul McCusker, pp. 7, 118;
  Andy Meyer, pp. 18, 21; Dusan Petricic, pp. 22, 32, 143, 144 (top); Steve Schulman, pp. 8 (e, g), 11,
  13 (left), 14 (#6), 16 (a), 44, 46, 58, 63, 64, 80, 89, 90, 144 (bottom); Tom Sperling, pp. 13 (right),
  14 (#5); Gary Torrisi, pp. 1 (#5), 3, 4, 14 (#3), 16 (b, c, d, e, f, g, h), 27, 28, 93, 94, 136.
Photo credits: p. 20 *(middle)* age fotostock/George White, *(bottom)* Chuck Pefley/Alamy; p. 59 *(left)*
  Brooks Kraft/Corbis, *(right)* Mike Blake/Reuters/Corbis; p. 88 *(left)* ThinkStock LLC/Index Stock
  Imagery, *(right)* Rebecca Cook/Reuters/Corbis; p. 89 *(top left)* Stockdisc/Getty Images, *(top right)*
  Rubberball/Getty Images, *(bottom left)* Michael Newman/PhotoEdit, *(bottom right)* Casa
  Productions/Corbis; p. 135 *(top left)* Courtesy of Mercedes-Benz USA, LLC, *(top middle)* Photo
  courtesy of Frank Zimmerman, *(top right)* Michael Newman/PhotoEdit, *(middle left)* Tibor
  Bognar/Corbis, *(middle center)* Royalty-Free/Corbis, *(middle right)* Bill Ross/Corbis, *(bottom left)*
  Paul A. Souders/Corbis, *(bottom middle)* Charles O'Rear/Corbis, *(bottom right)* Carl & Ann
  Purcell/Corbis.

ISBN: 0-13-147469-3 (Workbook)

LONGMAN ON THE **WEB**

Longman.com offers online resources for
teachers and students. Access our Companion
Websites, our online catalog, and our local
offices around the world.

Visit us at **longman.com.**

Printed in the United States of America
4 5 6 7 8 9 10—BAH—12 11 10 09 08

Contents

About the Author

Samuela Eckstut has taught ESL and EFL for over twenty-five years, in the United States, Greece, Italy, and England. Currently she is teaching at Boston University, Center for English Language and Orientation Programs (CELOP). She has authored or co-authored numerous texts for the teaching of English, notably *Strategic Reading 1, 2* and *3, What's in a Word? Reading and Vocabulary Building; In the Real World; First Impressions; Beneath the Surface; Widely Read;* and *Finishing Touches.*

Imperatives

1 | AFFIRMATIVE AND NEGATIVE IMPERATIVES

Look at the pictures. Circle the correct answers.

1. **a.** Park here.

   b. Don't park here. It's a bus stop.

2. **a.** Sit down.

   b. Don't sit down.

3. **a.** Close your books.

   b. Don't close your books.

4. **a.** Don't open the door.

   b. Please open the door.

5. **a.** Don't turn left. Turn right.

   b. Don't turn right. Turn left.

6. **a.** Open your eyes.

   b. Don't open your eyes.

2 | INSTRUCTIONS

Write instructions. Use the words in the box.

Answer	Circle	Look at	Read	Write
Ask	Listen to	Open	Underline	

1. _____*Open*_____ the book.

_____*Read*_____

_____

2. _____ the CD.

_____

3. _____ the board.

_____

4. _____ the teacher.

_____

_____

5. _____ the group.

_____

6. _____ the word *English*.

_____

_____

3 | NUMBERS (1–10)

Complete the sentences. Write the numbers.

$$\begin{array}{r} 3 \\ +\ 7 \\ \hline 10 \end{array} \qquad \begin{array}{r} 2 \\ +\ 6 \\ \hline 8 \end{array}$$

1. Three and ____*seven*____ is ten.

2. _____ and three is eight.

3. One and two is _____.

4. Nine and one is _____.

5. Two and _____ is eight.

6. Three and _____ is six.

7. _____ and five is six.

8. Seven and two is _____.

9. _____ and two is four.

10. Three and _____ is seven.

4 | NEW VOCABULARY

Write the word(s) next to the correct picture.

a bus stop	a restaurant	~~empty~~	turn left
a gas station	a truck	full	turn right

1. _____*full*_____

2. _____

3. _____

4. _____

(continued)

5. _____

6. _____

7. _____

8. _____

5 | EDITING

Correct these conversations. There are four mistakes. The first mistake is already corrected.

1. **A:** ~~No~~ *Don't* park here. It's a bus stop.

   B: Oh. OK.

2. **A:** You no go straight. Turn left.

   B: Got it.

3. **A:** Please don't you close the window. It's hot!

   B: Sure. No problem.

4. **A:** Drives one block. Then turn right.

   B: OK. Thanks.

6 | CONVERSATION COMPLETION

Complete the conversation. Use the words in the box. Don't look at your Student Book.

Avenue	drive	Indian	the truck
Don't park	the gas station	~~the restaurant~~	turn
Don't worry	Got it		

MARK: Is _____*the restaurant*_____ close? I'm hungry.
1.

STEVE: Yes, it is.

MARK: Is it good?

STEVE: _____. It's very good. It's
2.

_____.
3.

MARK: Great.

STEVE: Now _____ to the corner, and
4.

_____ left at Jackson Street.
5.

MARK: At _____?
6.

STEVE: Yes. Then go two blocks on Jackson.

MARK: _____.
7.

STEVE: OK. Turn right at the next corner.

MARK: At Third _____?
8.

STEVE: Yes. The restaurant is on the corner on your right.

MARK: Is that it?

STEVE: Yes, it is. _____ here. It's a bus
9.

stop. Park behind _____.
10.

MARK: OK . . . Uh, Steve? The restaurant is empty.

STEVE: Really? It's usually full.

MARK: Is that a sign on the door?

STEVE: Uh-huh . . . "Closed for vacation."

2 This is / These are; Subject Pronouns

1 | WORDS

Look at the people in Steve's family. Who are they? Use the words in the box.

brother	father	mother	son
daughter	husband	sister	wife

1. ___wife___

___mother___

2. ___husband___

___father___

3. _____

_____

4. _____

_____

_____

_____

5. _____

_____

6. _____

_____

7. _____

_____

8. _____

_____

2 | VOCABULARY

Complete the crossword puzzle.

Across

2.

7.

8.

9.

10.

11.

12.

13.

Down

1.

3.

4.

5.

6.

9.

3 | SUBJECT PRONOUNS

Complete the sentences with **I**, **he**, **she**, **it**, **we**, *or* **they**.

Marie-Claire is my friend. ___She___ is from Quebec. Quebec is a city in Canada. _____
1.   2.
is a nice city. Marie-Claire says, "_____ love Quebec. _____ is my home." _____
                                        3.   4.   5.
lives in Quebec with her husband, Eric. _____ is from New York. _____ are teachers. The
                                          6.   7.
school is near their home. _____ is a big school. Eric says, " _____ are new teachers. Our
                            8.   9.
students are new too. _____ are very nice."
                       10.

4 | THIS IS / THESE ARE

Look at the pictures. Match the sentences with the pictures.

a.

b.

c.

d.

✗

f.

g.

h.

___e___ **1.** This is a ticket.

_____ **2.** These are Jessica's children.

_____ **3.** This is my guitar.

_____ **4.** This is a book.

_____ **5.** These are my pets.

_____ **6.** These are my friends.

_____ **7.** These are my parents.

_____ **8.** This is my friend Pedro.

5 | QUESTIONS AND STATEMENTS WITH *THIS* AND *THESE*

Put the words in the correct order. Write sentences. Remember to add the correct capitalization.

1. book / this / your / is / ?   <u>*Is this your book?*</u>

2. pencil / this / your / is / .   _____

3. your / is / ticket / this / ?   _____

4. keys / are / these / your / .   _____

5. my / is / house / this / .   _____

6. is / apartment / your / this / ?   _____

7. your / these / friends / are / ?   _____

8. these / seats / your / are / .   _____

6 | THIS IS / THESE ARE

Complete the sentences. Circle the correct answers and write them on the lines.

1. These are my _____*parents*_____.

   a. parent   **(b.)** parents

2. This is my _____.

   a. brother   **b.** brothers

3. These are my _____.

   a. sister   **b.** sisters

4. These are my _____.

   a. friend   **b.** friends

5. This is my _____.

   a. partner   **b.** partners

6. This is my _____.

   a. class   **b.** classes

7 | EDITING

Correct these conversations. There are six mistakes. The first mistake is already corrected.

1. **A:** Is ~~these~~ *this* your ticket?

   B: Yes, it is.

2. **A:** These are your keys?

   B: Yes. Thank you.

3. **A:** This is my car.

   B: She is big.

4. **A:** This are *my* books.

   B: Oh. Sorry.

5. **A:** These are my pet.

   B: They're nice.

6. **A:** Is this your sister?

   B: Yes, her name is Mary. He is a teacher.

The Present of *Be*: Statements

1 | AFFIRMATIVE AND NEGATIVE STATEMENTS WITH *BE*

Look at the pictures. Put a check (✓) next to the true statements.

Mexico

Ecuador

Egypt

Canada

Brazil

Taiwan

_____ 1. I'm Huang-Ping Cho. I'm from Egypt.

_✓_ 2. This is Gabrielle Da Silva. She's from Brazil.

_____ 3. I'm Roberto Vargas Llosa. I'm not from Mexico.

_____ 4. These are Juan Perez and Carlos Santos. They are from Peru.

_____ 5. I'm Huang-Ping Cho. I'm not from Japan.

_____ 6. This is Melissa Lewis. She's from Australia.

_____ 7. These are Blanca Layana and Roberto Vargas Llosa. They aren't from Brazil.

_____ 8. This is Asma Narrif. She's from Egypt.

2 | AFFIRMATIVE AND NEGATIVE STATEMENTS WITH *BE*

Complete the sentences. Use **is** *or* **isn't**.

1. New York _____*isn't*_____ the capital of the United States.

2. Brasília _____*is*_____ the capital of Brazil.

3. Sydney _____ the capital of Australia.

4. Quebec _____ the capital of Canada.

5. Cairo _____ the capital of Egypt.

6. Rome _____ the capital of Italy.

7. Canberra _____ the capital of Australia.

8. Tokyo _____ the capital of Japan.

3 | AFFIRMATIVE STATEMENTS WITH *BE*

Complete the letter. Use **am**, **is**, *or* **are**.

January 21

Dear Mom and Dad,

Karen and I ___*are*___ in Sydney. It _____ warm here. It's 32°C today.
1.   2.

Sydney _____ a wonderful city. The Opera House _____ beautiful, and
3.   4.

the people _____ friendly.
5.

We _____ at the Garden Hotel. The rooms _____ big but a little
6.   7.

expensive. Karen _____ in the hotel room now. I _____ at a very nice
8.   9.

restaurant. The food _____ delicious.
10.

Love,

Paul

4 | CONTRACTIONS OF AFFIRMATIVE AND NEGATIVE STATEMENTS WITH *BE*

Rewrite the sentences with the full forms of the contractions.

1. I'm from Ecuador. _I am from Ecuador._

2. It's beautiful there. _____

3. She isn't sad. _____

4. We're not here on business. _____

5. You're friendly. _____

6. They aren't from Seattle. _____

5 | CONTRACTIONS OF AFFIRMATIVE AND NEGATIVE STATEMENTS WITH *BE*

Rewrite the sentences with contractions.

1. It is not hot. _It's not hot._ OR _It isn't hot._

2. We are from Tokyo. _____

3. They are not here. _____

4. I am not the teacher. _____

5. He is my cousin. _____

6. You are from here. _____

6 | AFFIRMATIVE AND NEGATIVE STATEMENTS WITH *BE*

Circle the correct words to make true statements.

1. The people (are)/ aren't on vacation.

   They are /(aren't) at school.

2. The street is / isn't dirty.

   It 's / isn't clean.

(continued)

3. The elephant <u>is / isn't</u> small.

   It <u>'s / isn't</u> big.

4. I <u>'m / 'm not</u> a student.

   I <u>'m / 'm not</u> a teacher.

5. The coffee <u>is / isn't</u> delicious.

   It <u>'s / isn't</u> awful.

6. We <u>'re / 're not</u> cold.

   We <u>'re / 're not</u> hot.

7 | EDITING

Correct these conversations. There are ten mistakes. The first two mistakes are already corrected.

1. **A:** ~~Are~~ *Is* Mark from around here?

   B: Yes, ~~they~~ *he* is.

2. **A:** The food good?

   B: Is delicious.

3. **A:** This my cousin.

   B: Are she a student?

4. **A:** Be you from Mexico?

   B: No, we're are from Peru.

5. **A:** Your cousins Amy and Mary are here on vacation?

   B: No, they here on business.

8 | CONVERSATION COMPLETION

Complete the conversation. Use the words in the box. Don't look at your Student Book.

am	capital	delicious	I	It's	They're
Australia	clean	from	is	not	~~This~~

MARK: Hi, Steve.

STEVE: Hi, Mark. _____*This*_____ is my cousin Amy, and this _____ her friend
       1.   2.
       Jenny. _____ here on vacation.
               3.

MARK: Hi. Nice to meet you.

AMY: Nice to meet you too.

MARK: So you're _____ from around here?
                  4.

AMY: No. We're from _____.
                     5.

MARK: Australia? That's pretty far away. Are you from the _____?
                                                            6.

AMY: No. We're from Sydney. How about you? Are you _____ Seattle?
                                                    7.

MARK: Yes, I _____.
              8.

AMY: Jenny and I love Seattle. It's a beautiful and _____ city. The people are
                                                     9.
     friendly. And the coffee is _____.
                                  10.

MARK: How's Sydney?

AMY: _____ a wonderful city—and not just because _____ live
      11.   12.
     there!

4 That is / Those are; Possessive Adjectives; Plural Nouns

1 | WORDS AND EXPRESSIONS

Look at the pictures. Match the sentences with the pictures.

a.   b.  c.  d.

e.  f.  g.  h.

_c_ **1.** That's a stadium.

____ **2.** That's an ant. It's tiny.

____ **3.** That's his camera.

____ **4.** Those are my binoculars.

____ **5.** Those are tall buildings.

____ **6.** That's an elephant. It's huge.

____ **7.** That's a museum.

____ **8.** Those are shapes.

2 | THIS, THAT, THESE, AND THOSE

Read the conversations. Circle the correct words to complete them.

1. **A:** What's this /(that) over there?

   B: This / That? The Space Needle.

2. **A:** Wow! What are these / those big buildings over there?

   B: These / Those are the stadiums.

3. **A:** Excuse me. Is this / these your seat?

   B: Yes, it is. Sorry. But those / that seat over there is free.

4. **A:** These / This is a very nice photo. Are this / these your children?

   B: Yes, they are. These / That are my sons, Juan and Pedro.

5. **A:** Mark, this / that is my friend Jenny. She's from Sydney.

   B: Hi, Jenny. Is this / that your first vacation in Seattle?

3 | SINGULAR AND PLURAL NOUNS

Write the sentences in the singular.

1. Those women are from Brazil. *That woman is from Brazil.*

2. Those cars are from Italy. _____

3. Those children are from Canada. _____

4. Those boys are from Egypt. _____

5. Those dishes are from Austria. _____

4 | SINGULAR AND PLURAL NOUNS

Write the sentences in the plural.

1. That man is from Brazil. *Those men are from Brazil.*

2. That person is from Mexico. _____

3. That girl is from Japan. _____

4. That glass is from Austria. _____

5. That computer is from the United States. _____

5 | POSSESSIVE ADJECTIVES

Complete the story. Use **my**, **his**, **her**, **our**, *or* **their**.

That's me and _____*my*_____ family. Those are _____ sisters. _____
⎯⎯⎯⎯ 1.   2.   3.

names are Kate, Ann, and Ruth. And that's _____ little brother. _____ name is
                                                                    4.   5.

Sam. _____ parents aren't in the picture. Kate and _____ husband have one
         6.   7.

daughter. _____ name is Amy.
                 8.

6 | SUBJECT PRONOUNS AND POSSESSIVE ADJECTIVES

Complete the conversations. Circle the correct answers. Write the words on the lines.

1. **A:** My name's Serena.

   B: _____*It's*_____ a beautiful name.

      a. Its   **(b.)** It's

2. **A:** _____ wrong.

      a. Your   **b.** You're

   B: No, I'm not.

3. **A:** Steve and Amy aren't here.

   B: But _____ car is here.

      a. their   **b.** they're

4. **A:** _____ car's nice.

      a. Your   **b.** You're

   B: Thanks.

5. **A:** Are those your CDs?

   B: No, _____ my brother's CDs.

      a. their   **b.** they're

6. **A:** Is that your cat?

   B: Yes, _____ name is Ernie.

      a. its   **b.** it's

7 | EDITING

Correct these conversations. There are ten mistakes. The first two mistakes are already corrected.

1. **A:** Is that your ~~books~~? *(book)*
   B: Yes, ~~its~~ is. *(it)*

2. **A:** Are those you're children?

   B: No, they're my brother's child.

3. **A:** Are that your glasses?

   B: No, they're my sunglass.

4. **A:** Those person are teachers.

   B: His names are Steve Beck and Annie Macintosh.

5. **A:** That is your cousin?

   B: Yes, she name is Jessica.

8 | CONVERSATION COMPLETION

Complete the conversations. Use the words in the box. Don't look at your Student Book.

binoculars	a great idea	How about	It's	~~that~~	those
building	her	huge	its	That's	your

AMY: So is _____that_____ it?
1.

STEVE: Yes. That's the Space Needle. _____ a
2.

picture?

AMY: Sure. It's too bad Jenny isn't here, but I have

_____ camera.
3.

STEVE: Come on. Let's go.

* * * * *

AMY: Wow! What are _____ big buildings?
4.

STEVE: They're the stadiums. Here, look through my

_____.
5.

AMY: They're _____! And those are people next
6.

to them. They look so tiny.

STEVE: Yes. Now look that way. _____ the
7.

University of Washington.

AMY: That's _____ university, right?
8.

STEVE: Yes, it is. OK, now look down. Look at that colored

_____.
9.

AMY: What is it? The colors are beautiful, but

_____ shape is really unusual.
10.

STEVE: That's the EMP. _____ a music museum.
11.

It belongs to Paul Allen. It's his "baby."

AMY: Let's go see it.

STEVE: That's _____.
12.

The Present of *Be*: Yes / No Questions, Questions with *Who* and *What*

1 | YES / NO QUESTIONS WITH *BE*; QUESTIONS WITH *WHO* AND *WHAT*

Write two conversations. Use the sentences in the box.

Diaz.	Is she a good teacher?
Travel books.	What does she write?
She's a writer.	~~Is that your wife?~~
Yes. Her name's Ellen.	What does she do?
Yes. And she's friendly too.	~~Who's that woman?~~
That's Amy. She's my teacher.	What's her last name?

Conversation 1

Conversation 2

Conversation 1

A: _____Who's that woman?_____

B: _____

A: _____

B: _____

A: _____

B: _____

Conversation 2

A: _____Is that your wife?_____

B: _____

A: _____

B: _____

A: _____

B: _____

21

2 | WORDS AND EXPRESSIONS

Look at the pictures. Circle the correct answers.

1.

Is he a cashier?

a. Yes, he is.

(b.) No, he isn't.

2.

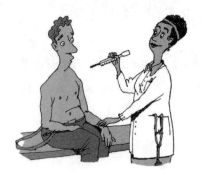

Is she a police officer?

a. Yes, she is.

b. No, she isn't.

3.

Is he a mechanic?

a. Yes, he is.

b. No, he isn't.

4.

Is he a nurse?

a. Yes, he is.

b. No, he isn't.

3 | YES / NO QUESTIONS WITH *BE;* QUESTIONS WITH *WHO* AND *WHAT*

Complete the conversations. Put the words in the correct order. Write questions.

1. A: you / student / a / Are / ?

  Are you a student?

 B: Yes, I am.

2. A: she / Is / sister / your / ?

  _____

 B: No, she isn't. She's my cousin.

3. A: that / Who / is / woman / ?

_____

B: She's my teacher.

4. A: father / an / your / Is / engineer / ?

_____

B: No, he isn't. He's a police officer.

5. A: their / name / is / What / last / ?

_____

B: It's Lee.

6. A: do / friend / does / What / your / ?

_____

B: Steve? Oh, he's a nurse.

4 | SHORT ANSWERS WITH THE PRESENT OF *BE*

Answer the questions. Write true short answers with the correct form of **be**.

1. Are you a student? _Yes, I am._ _____

2. Are you single? _____

3. Are you nervous? _____

4. Is your teacher married? _____

5. Is your teacher from Canada? _____

6. Is it hot now? _____

7. Are your classmates happy? _____

8. Are you and your classmates friends? _____

5 | QUESTIONS WITH *WHO* AND *WHAT*

Complete the chart. Write short answers.

	QUESTIONS	LONG ANSWERS	SHORT ANSWERS
1.	What's your name?	It's Mary.	Mary.
2.	Who's that student?	That's Ben.	
3.	Who are they?	They're my grandchildren.	
4.	What's that?	It's a key.	

6 | QUESTIONS WITH *WHO* AND *WHAT*

Complete the chart. Write long answers.

	QUESTIONS	SHORT ANSWERS	LONG ANSWERS
1.	What's your name?	Mary.	It's Mary.
2.	Who's that man?	My brother.	
3.	What's the capital of Australia?	Canberra.	
4.	Who's the teacher of this class?	Lynn Martin.	

7 | EDITING

Correct the conversations. There are ten mistakes. The first mistake is already corrected.

1. A: ~~Who's~~ *What's* her last name?

   B: Martinez.

2. A: You and Joe married?

   B: Yes, we're.

3. A: Who be that boy?

   B: That my son.

4. A: Who is the capital of the United States?

   B: Is Washington, D.C.

5. A: That woman your mother?

   B: Yes, she's.

6. A: Bob a travel agent is?

   B: No, he isn't.

8 | CONVERSATION COMPLETION

Complete the conversations. Use the words in the box. Don't look at your Student Book.

~~Are~~	does	He's	it	she's	Who's
Boy	Her	Is	she	What	you

STEVE: Mark?

MARK: Steve! _____Are_____ you here for the wedding?
　　　　　　　　　　 1.

STEVE: Yes, I am. Amanda is my cousin. What about

　　　 _____?
　　　　　　 2.

MARK: Josh and I are good friends from school.

　　　 _____, this is a great wedding.
　　　　　　 3.

STEVE: Yes, _____ is.
　　　　　　　　 4.

KATHY: _____ that man with Steve?
　　　　　　 5.

AMANDA: His name is Mark. He and Josh are friends.

KATHY: Hmm. _____ he single?
　　　　　　　　 6.

AMANDA: Yes, he is.

KATHY: What _____ he do?
　　　　　　　　 7.

AMANDA: _____ a student and a writer.
　　　　 8.

KATHY: What kind of writer?

AMANDA: He writes travel books.

MARK: Who's that woman with Amanda?

STEVE: _____ name is Kathy.
　　　　　 9.

MARK: Is _____ married?
　　　　　　　 10.

STEVE: No, _____ not.
　　　　　　　　 11.

MARK: Hmmm . . . _____ does she do?
　　　　　　　　　　　 12.

STEVE: She's a travel agent.

6 The Present of *Be*: Questions with *Where*; Prepositions of Place

1 | WORDS AND EXPRESSIONS

One word is spelled wrong. Write the word correctly. Don't look at your Student Book.

1. supermarket

   apartement building

   bank

   _____apartment building_____

2. movie theater

   park

   hospitol

   _____

3. gym

   resterant

   post office

   _____

4. museam

   supermarket

   restaurant

   _____

5. libary

   gym

   post office

   _____

6. coffee shop

   movie thaeter

   library

   _____

2 | PREPOSITIONS OF PLACE

Look at the map. Read the sentences. Write **T** *for* True *or* **F** *for* False.

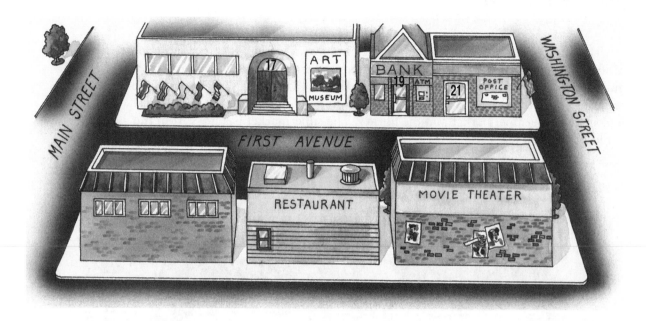

___F___ **1.** The movie theater is across from the restaurant.

___T___ **2.** The post office is across from the movie theater.

_____ **3.** The bank is between the post office and the art museum.

_____ **4.** The art museum is between the restaurant and the movie theater.

_____ **5.** The art museum is next to the post office.

_____ **6.** The restaurant is on Washington Street.

_____ **7.** The post office is at number 21 First Avenue.

_____ **8.** The art museum is across from the restaurant.

3 | PREPOSITIONS OF PLACE

Read the description and look at the picture. Write the correct place names next to the numbers for the buildings.

The bank is at the corner of Tenth Street and West Avenue. It's next to the post office. The movie theater is at the corner of Ninth Street and East Avenue. The art museum is on Ninth Street next to the movie theater. The park is across from the restaurant and the theater. The apartment building is across from the post office. It's between the supermarket and the library. The supermarket is across from the bank.

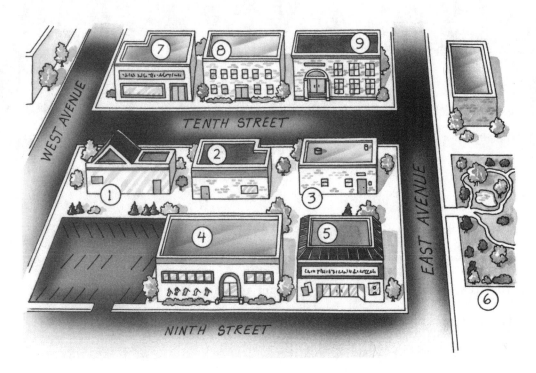

1. _____bank_____   6. _____

2. _____   7. _____

3. _____   8. _____

4. _____   9. _____

5. _____

4 | THE PRESENT OF *BE:* QUESTIONS WITH *WHERE*

Write a question for each answer. Use **where** *in each question.*

1. **A:** *Where's Ana from?* OR *Where is Ana from?*

   B: Ana? She's from Brazil.

2. **A:** _____

   B: Mr. and Mrs. Lin? They're from Australia.

3. **A:** _____

   B: The doctors? They're from Mexico.

4. **A:** _____

   B: Paul? He's from Australia.

5. **A:** _____

   B: I'm from the United States.

5 | ORDINAL NUMBERS

Complete the chart.

	NUMBER	WORD	ORDINAL NUMBER	ORDINAL WORD
1.	4	*four*	4th	*fourth*
2.	6	six		
3.	1			first
4.	9	nine		
5.	8		8th	
6.	2			second
7.	3	three		
8.	7		7th	
9.	10			tenth
10.	5		5th	

6 | ORDINAL NUMBERS

Look at the sign. Answer the questions. Spell out the ordinal numbers.

MAIN STREET MEDICAL BUILDING	Floor
Doctor Bell	5
Doctor Chan	1
Doctor Din	3
Doctor Lugo	4
Doctor Peterson	6
Doctor Shore	2

1. Where's Doctor Bell's office? _It's on the fifth floor._

2. Where's Doctor Chan's office? _____

3. Where's Doctor Din's office? _____

4. Where's Doctor Lugo's office? _____

5. Where's Doctor Peterson's office? _____

6. Where's Doctor Shore's office? _____

7 | EDITING

Correct the e-mail messages. There are seven mistakes. The first mistake is already corrected.

Subj: Phone number and address
Date: Friday, June 10
From: BobMcDonald@MU.edu
To: PLM@MU.edu

Hi, Paula,

                                                                    where's
What's your phone number, and ~~what's~~ your apartment? Is it on Main Street? And what

floor is your apartment in?

Bob

Subj: Re: Phone number and address
Date: Saturday, June 11
From: PLM@MU.edu
To: BobMcDonald@MU.edu

Hi, Bob,

My phone number 555-0900. My apartment isn't at Main Street. It's on 212 Park

Avenue. Take the number 12 bus. My apartment building is next the post office, and

my apartment is on the nine floor.

Paula

UNIT 7

The Past of *Be*: Statements, Yes / No Questions

1 | AFFIRMATIVE AND NEGATIVE STATEMENTS WITH THE PAST OF *BE*

*Read the sentences. Write **T** for True or **F** for False.*

_____ 1. I was late for class yesterday.

_____ 2. I wasn't at the library last night.

_____ 3. A friend was with me yesterday.

_____ 4. My teacher wasn't at school yesterday.

_____ 5. My friends and I were at a movie yesterday.

_____ 6. My family and I were at home last night.

_____ 7. My friends were at my home last night.

_____ 8. My classmates weren't happy in the last English class.

2 | AFFIRMATIVE STATEMENTS WITH THE PAST OF *BE*

Look at the pictures. Match the sentences with the pictures.

a.

b.

c.

d.

___*e*___ 1. The movie was exciting.

_____ 2. The television show was funny.

_____ 3. The television show was scary.

_____ 4. The movie was interesting.

_____ 5. The television show was boring.

3 | AFFIRMATIVE AND NEGATIVE STATEMENTS WITH THE PAST OF *BE*

Complete the sentences. Use **was**, **wasn't**, **were**, *or* **weren't** *and* **yesterday**.

1. Jack's at home today, but   *he wasn't at home yesterday.*

2. Jenny wasn't in class today, but   *she was in class yesterday.*

3. I'm happy today, but _____

4. It's cold today, but _____

5. The children are not at a soccer game today, but _____

6. We aren't tired today, but _____

7. The streets aren't crowded today, but _____

8. You're at the library today, but _____

9. I'm not home today, but _____

10. The boys are at the movies today, but _____

4 | THE PAST OF *BE*: AFFIRMATIVE AND NEGATIVE STATEMENTS

Complete Kathy's diary. Use **was**, **wasn't**, **were**, *or* **weren't**.

April 15

   Yesterday _____was_____ great. I _____ alone. I _____
                      1.   **2.**   **3.**
with Mark. We _____ at a movie. The movie _____
                       4.   **5.**
Frankenstein's Uncle. It _____ really funny.
                             6.
   Amanda and Josh _____ with me and Mark. They stopped by
                             7.
my house, but I _____ home. Amanda doesn't know Mark and I
                      8.
_____ together.
    9.

5 | QUESTIONS AND SHORT ANSWERS WITH THE PAST OF *BE*

Look at the pictures. Write questions. Use the words in parentheses and the correct form of **be**. *Then write short answers.*

1. (Bill and Steve / at a movie / last night)

   Were Bill and Steve at a movie last night?   *No, they weren't.*

   Where *were they?*   *At a concert.*

2. (Jeremy / at a soccer game / yesterday)

   _____   _____

3. (Tim and Jessica / at a play / yesterday)

   _____   _____

4. (Judy / at a party / last night)

_____   _____

Where _____   _____

5. (Mark / at a soccer game / yesterday)

_____   _____

Where _____   _____

6. (Amy, Steve, and Jenny / at a party / last night)

_____   _____

6 | EDITING

Correct the conversations. There are seven mistakes. The first mistake is already corrected.

1. A: ~~They were~~ at home yesterday?
    Were they

    B: Yes, they was.

2. A: Hi. How it going?

    B: Great.

3. A: Were the movie funny yesterday?

    B: No, it isn't.

4. A: Where were you the last night?

    B: Was at home.

7 | CONVERSATION COMPLETION

Complete the conversation. Use the words in the box. Don't look at your Student Book.

alone	great	it	movies	was	were
funny	How's	last	~~This~~	wasn't	weren't

KATHY: Hello?

AMANDA: Hi, Kathy. _____This_____ is Amanda.
                             1.

KATHY: Hi, Amanda. _____ it going?
                                     2.

AMANDA: Fine. Hey, Josh and I were at your house _____
                                              3.

night, but you _____ there. Or _____
                      4.   5.

you asleep?

KATHY: Actually, I _____ at home last night. I was at the
                           6.

_____.
     7.

AMANDA: Were you _____?
                      8.

KATHY: Uh, no. I _____ with . . . someone. The movie
                    9.

was _____. Really exciting. And _____
           10.   11.

too.

AMANDA: Really! What movie was _____?
                                   12.

KATHY: *Frankenstein's Uncle.*

The Past of *Be*:
Wh- Questions

1 | *WH-* QUESTIONS WITH THE PAST OF *BE*

Complete the questions. Use the words in the box. Some words will be used more than once.

How	How long	What	When	Where	Who

1. **A:** _____How_____ was the weather yesterday?

   B: It was cool and sunny.

2. **A:** _____ were you in Spain?

   B: Two weeks ago.

3. **A:** _____ were you Tuesday afternoon?

   B: I was at a baseball game.

4. **A:** _____ were you with last weekend?

   B: My parents. They came to visit.

5. **A:** _____ was your weekend?

   B: It was a lot of fun.

6. **A:** _____ movie was it?

   B: It was *A Night in Paris*.

7. **A:** _____ was the concert?

   B: About two hours.

8. **A:** _____ was at the game with you?

   B: My brother.

2 | THE PAST OF *BE: WH-* QUESTIONS AND LONG ANSWERS

Put the words in the correct order. Write questions. Then write true long answers.

1. Saturday / you / on / were / Where / ?

   Where were you on Saturday?

   I was at the library.

2. class / your / How / was / English / long / ?

   _____

   _____

3. you / at / the / When / supermarket / were / ?

   _____

   _____

4. was / weather / the / How / yesterday / ?

   _____

   _____

5. yesterday / you / Where / were / ?

   _____

   _____

6. you / Who / with / last / weekend / were / ?

   _____

   _____

3 | THE PAST OF *BE: WH-* QUESTIONS AND SHORT ANSWERS

Read Jason's postcard. Answer Mark's questions. Use short answers.

> July 4
>
> Hi, James,
>
> It's great here in San Francisco. I'm here on vacation for five days with my brother and sister. The weather isn't great. It's cool and rainy, but we're having fun. See you next week.
>
> Jason
>
> James O' Malley
> 111 Washington Ave.
> Seattle, WA 98101

MARK: James said you went on vacation. When did you go?

JASON: <u>Last week.</u>
              1.

MARK: How was your vacation?

JASON: _____
              2.

MARK: Where were you?

JASON: _____
              3.

MARK: Who were you with?

JASON: _____
              4.

MARK: How long were you there?

JASON: _____
              5.

MARK: How was the weather?

JASON: _____
              6.

4 | WORDS AND EXPRESSIONS

Look at the weather information. Answer the questions.

CITY	°F	°C	CONDITIONS
London	45	7	R
Mexico City	98	37	R
New York	20	−5	S
Quebec	−10	−23	C
Sydney	75	24	S
Tokyo	55	13	W

☀ YESTERDAY'S WEATHER

C = cloudy   R = rainy   S = sunny   W = windy

1. How was the weather in London yesterday? *It was cool and rainy.* _____

2. How was the weather in Mexico City yesterday? _____

3. How was the weather in New York yesterday? _____

4. How was the weather in Quebec yesterday? _____

5. How was the weather in Sydney yesterday? _____

6. How was the weather in Tokyo yesterday? _____

5 | EDITING

Correct the conversations. There are six mistakes. The first mistake is already corrected.

1. **A:** Where ~~you were~~ *were you* last night?

   B: I was at a soccer game.

2. **A:** Who were the students?

   B: They were with their teacher.

3. **A:** How long class?

   B: Two hours.

4. **A:** How was the weather?

   B: Was sunny and warm.

5. **A:** When was they here?

   B: Last Friday.

6. **A:** Who movie was it?

   B: *Star Wars.*

6 | CONVERSATION COMPLETION

Complete the conversation. Use the words in the box. Don't look at your Student Book.

cool	long	this	~~vacation~~	weather	wonderful
food	Remember	tour	was	Who	you

JASON: Hi, Mark.

MARK: Hey, Jason.

JASON: Welcome back. How was your ___*vacation*___?
1.

MARK: Great.

JASON: You look good. Where were _____?
2.

MARK: In Spain.

JASON: Nice. How _____ were you there?
3.

MARK: Ten days. Ten _____ days.
4.

JASON: That's a long vacation. My parents were there last month. It was hot. How was the

_____?
5.

MARK: Hot and sunny. But it was _____ at the beach.
6.

JASON: And the _____?
7.

MARK: Delicious.

JASON: So . . . were you on a _____?
8.

MARK: No, but I _____ with a guide.
9.

JASON: A guide? _____ was your guide?
10.

MARK: _____ Kathy? At Amanda's wedding? The travel agent?
11.

JASON: Sure.

MARK: Well, she's in Barcelona _____ month. She was my guide.
12.

JASON: You lucky man!

UNIT

9 The Simple Present: Statements

1 | AFFIRMATIVE AND NEGATIVE STATEMENTS WITH THE SIMPLE PRESENT

Complete the sentences. Circle the correct answers. Write the words on the lines.

1. Jessica _____has_____ a brother.

    a. have   **b.** having   **c.** has

2. Jessica and Tim _____ three children.

    a. having   **b.** have   **c.** has

3. Steve doesn't _____ children.

    a. have   **b.** has   **c.** having

4. Mary _____ with her children, Jessica and Steve.

    a. no lives   **b.** doesn't live   **c.** is no live

5. Mary _____ with her husband, Bill.

    a. live   **b.** is live   **c.** lives

6. Steve _____ at a university.

    a. work   **b.** works   **c.** working

7. Jessica and Tim _____ at home.

    a. doesn't work   **b.** no work   **c.** don't work

8. Jeremy _____ computer games.

    a. likes   **b.** like   **c.** is like

2 | AFFIRMATIVE STATEMENTS WITH THE SIMPLE PRESENT

Complete the sentences. Use the correct forms of the verbs in the box.

babysit	like	play	report	sing	teach	~~write~~

1. Mark is a writer. He _____*writes*_____ travel books.

2. Jessica is a news reporter. She _____ the news.

3. Steve is a teacher. He _____ journalism.

4. Nick goes online a lot. He _____ computers.

5. Kelly is a babysitter. She _____ for the Olsons.

6. Shakira is a singer. She _____ in Spanish and English.

7. Ronaldo and Mario are soccer players. They _____ soccer.

3 | THE SIMPLE PRESENT: NEGATIVE VERBS

Complete the sentences. Use negative verbs.

1. We want pizza, but we _____*don't want*_____ dessert.

2. The restaurant has spaghetti, but it _____ fish.

3. I speak Spanish, but I _____ Portuguese.

4. Kelly and Ken need a computer, but they _____ a TV.

5. We like coffee, but we _____ tea.

6. My sister wants a dog, but she _____ a cat.

7. You have mistakes in Exercise 1, but you _____ mistakes in Exercise 2.

8. Jack teaches on Mondays and Wednesdays, but he _____ on Tuesdays or Thursdays.

9. It rains a lot in Seattle, but it _____ a lot in Los Angeles.

4 | AFFIRMATIVE AND NEGATIVE STATEMENTS WITH THE SIMPLE PRESENT

Look at the pictures. Write true statements about yourself.

1.

eat breakfast

I eat breakfast. OR *I don't eat breakfast.*

2.

drink coffee

_____

3.

read newspapers

_____

4.

go online

_____

5.

read novels

_____

6.

study a lot

_____

5 | AFFIRMATIVE AND NEGATIVE STATEMENTS WITH THE SIMPLE PRESENT

Write the correct verb forms. Use the verbs in parentheses.

I _____*have*_____ a brother and a sister. My sister and I _____ alike, but
   1. (have)   **2. (look)**

my brother and I _____ alike. My sister and I _____ brown hair and
            3. (not look)   **4. (have)**

brown eyes. My brother _____ black hair and blue eyes. My sister and I both
                       5. (have)

_____. My sister _____ in an office. I _____ in a
  6. (work)   **7. (work)**   **8. (work)**

library. My brother _____. He _____ to school, and on weekends he
                9. (not work)   **10. (go)**

_____ cars. He _____ cars, but he _____ school. At
  11. (fix)   **12. (love)**   **13. (not love)**

work and at school, we _____ English, but we _____ English at
                14. (speak)   **15. (not speak)**

home. At home we _____ Spanish. That's because my parents _____
         16. (speak)   **17. (not come)**

from the United States. My father _____ from Peru and my mother
                      18. (come)

_____ from Mexico. My mother _____ English and Spanish, but my
  19. (come)   **20. (speak)**

father _____ English.
      21. (not speak)

6 | EDITING

Correct the description of Judy's family. There are ten mistakes. The first mistake is already corrected.

                         lives
    My brother, Ken, ~~live~~ with my parents. They lives in a big house. My father have a new car.

He cleans his car every day. Ken not have a new car. His car is old. It don't run, but he love it. My

mother no love cars. She love her garden. She work in it every Saturday and Sunday. I doesn't see

my family often, but we talk on the weekend.

7 | CONVERSATION COMPLETION

Complete the conversation. Use the words in the box. Don't look at your Student Book.

doesn't	go	hair	likes	look	teaches
eyes	goes	~~like~~	lives	sounds	watch

JUDY: I need more coffee. Would you ____*like*____ some?
1.

MARK: Yes, please.

JUDY: Here you _____.
2.

MARK: Thanks.

JUDY: Oh! New photos?

MARK: Yep . . . Look at this one. This is my brother, Nick. He

_____ in Kenya. He _____ English
3.   **4.**

there.

JUDY: In Kenya? Wow! . . . You _____ alike.
5.

MARK: I know. We both have dark brown _____ and
6.

green _____.
7.

JUDY: And you're both tall.

MARK: But we're different in a lot of ways.

JUDY: How?

MARK: Well, I like people and parties. Nick _____
8.

computers. I don't like computers, and Nick

_____ like parties.
9.

JUDY: Anything else?

MARK: Uh-huh. I speak Chinese. Nick speaks Swahili. I read

newspapers and magazines. Nick reads novels and

grammar books. I _____ DVDs almost every
10.

night, but Nick _____ online. He e-mails me
11.

a lot.

JUDY: Yeah? He _____ interesting.
12.

The Simple Present: Yes / No Questions

1 | YES / NO QUESTIONS WITH THE SIMPLE PRESENT

*Are the questions for Ben or for Jessica? Write **B** or **J**.*

Jessica   Ben

__J__ **1.** Do your children clean their rooms?

__B__ **2.** Does your father play basketball with you?

_____ **3.** Does your husband cook?

_____ **4.** Does your mother drive you to school?

_____ **5.** Do your brother and sister have homework?

_____ **6.** Does your husband drive to work?

_____ **7.** Do your parents help you with your homework?

_____ **8.** Do you visit your grandparents on the weekend?

_____ **9.** Does your brother teach at a university?

_____ **10.** Do your brother and sister play games with you?

2 | *YES / NO* **QUESTIONS AND SHORT ANSWERS WITH THE SIMPLE PRESENT**

Match the questions and answers.

_d_ **1.** Do you sleep every day?   **a.** No, it doesn't.

____ **2.** Do people in Japan speak Japanese?   **b.** Yes, it does.

____ **3.** Does it snow in Canada?   **c.** No, I don't.

____ **4.** Do you read novels in English?   ~~d.~~ Yes, I do.

____ **5.** Does the sun shine at night?   **e.** No, they don't.

____ **6.** Do teachers do homework?   **f.** Yes, they do.

3 | **SHORT ANSWERS WITH THE SIMPLE PRESENT**

Look at the chart. Answer the questions. Use short answers.

DO THEY LIKE . . . ?	KEN	JUDY	NICK	AMY
chocolate	yes	yes	no	yes
computer games	yes	no	yes	yes
plays	no	no	yes	no
music	no	yes	yes	yes
novels	yes	no	no	yes

1. Does Ken like chocolate? _Yes, he does._____

2. Does Ken like plays? _No, he doesn't._____

3. Does Amy like plays? _____

4. Do Nick and Judy like novels? _____

5. Does Judy like computer games? _____

6. Do Nick and Amy like computer games? _____

7. Does Judy like chocolate? _____

8. Do you like plays? _____

9. Do you like computer games? _____

4 | *YES / NO* QUESTIONS WITH THE SIMPLE PRESENT

Read the statements. Write yes / no questions in the simple present. Use the words in parentheses.

1. Jeremy doesn't play baseball.

   (basketball?) *Does he play basketball?* _____

2. Jessica doesn't work on Saturday.

   (on Sunday?) _____

3. Mark doesn't speak Spanish.

   (Japanese?) _____

4. Tim and Jessica don't have a dog.

   (cat?) _____

5. Judy doesn't know Amanda.

   (Kathy?) _____

6. Mary and Bill don't need a new clock.

   (a new radio?) _____

7. The school doesn't have a gym.

   (library?) _____

8. I don't speak English at home.

   (Portuguese?) _____

5 | *YES / NO* QUESTIONS AND SHORT ANSWERS WITH THE SIMPLE PRESENT

Write questions. Then write short answers. Use the information in parentheses and the simple present.

1. A: *Does Kathy like Mark?* _____

   B: *Yes, she does.* _____ (Kathy likes Mark.)

2. A: _____

   B: _____ (Mark needs a haircut.)

3. A: _____

   B: _____ (Steve knows a good hairstylist.)

(continued)

4. A: _____

   B: _____ (You don't like coffee.)

5. A: _____

   B: _____ (Mark speaks Chinese.)

6. A: _____

   B: _____ (Nick goes online and e-mails Mark.)

7. A: _____

   B: _____ (It doesn't rain a lot in September.)

8. A: _____

   B: _____ (Judy doesn't want coffee.)

9. A: _____

   B: _____ (Steve needs an appointment.)

6 | STATEMENTS AND *YES / NO* QUESTIONS WITH THE SIMPLE PRESENT

Complete the statements and yes / no *questions in the simple present. Use the words in parentheses. Use* **do** *or* **does** *where needed.*

ANNIE: _____*We want*_____ a gift for our brother.
　　　　　　1. (we / want)

SALESPERSON: _____ novels?
　　　　　　　　2. (he / read)

BEN: No, he doesn't.

SALESPERSON: _____ to CDs?
　　　　　　　　3. (your brother / listen)

ANNIE: Yeah. _____ a good idea.
　　　　　　　　4. (that / be)

SALESPERSON: What kind of music? _____ classical?
　　　　　　　　　　　　　　　　5. (you / like)

ANNIE: Yeah. _____ classical.
　　　　　　　6. (I / love)

BEN: But _____ classical.
　　　　　　7. (Jeremy / not like)

_____ a jazz CD?
8. (you / have)

_____ jazz.
9. (Jeremy / love)

7 | EDITING

Correct the conversations. There are eight mistakes. The first mistake is already corrected.

1. **A:** ~~You~~ *Do you* know Jeremy?

   B: No. Who is he?

2. **A:** Does your grandmother plays the guitar?

   B: Yes, she is.

3. **A:** Your three friends do play basketball?

   B: One friend play basketball. The other two play soccer.

4. **A:** *Focus on Grammar* have a lot of grammar practice?

   B: Yes, it has.

5. **A:** Do you and the other students like this book?

   B: No, we don't like.

8 | CONVERSATION COMPLETION

Complete the conversation. Use the words in the box. Don't look at your Student Book.

charge	have	know	need	reasonable	thinks
haircut	Hold on	like	Nothing much	think	~~What's~~

STEVE: Hello.

MARK: Hi, Steve. This is Mark.

STEVE: Hey, Mark. _____*What's*_____ up?
                              1.

MARK: _____. Kathy _____ I
              2.   3.

   need a haircut. I'm not so sure. But do you

   _____ a good barber?
         4.

STEVE: Yes. At least I like him. But he's not a barber. He's a

   hairstylist. His name is Marcello.

MARK: Oh. Does he _____ a lot?
                            5.

(continued)

STEVE: No, he doesn't. He's very _____, but
6.
he's pretty busy. You _____ an
7.
appointment.

MARK: Well, then, do you _____ his phone
8.
number?

STEVE: I think so. _____. I'll get it . . . It's
9.
306-555-0908. Make an appointment, Mark. I think
Kathy's right. You need a _____.
10.

MARK: Do you really _____ so? I kind of
11.
_____ my hair this way. But thanks for
12.
the number.

STEVE: No problem. Bye.

MARK: Bye.

The Simple Present: *Wh-* Questions

1 | WH- QUESTIONS WITH THE SIMPLE PRESENT

Match the questions and answers.

__d__ **1.** What time do you wake up?

_____ **2.** Where do you catch the bus?

_____ **3.** How do you know Amanda?

_____ **4.** Who do you live with?

_____ **5.** What do you do after class?

_____ **6.** Why do you take the bus to work?

_____ **7.** How late do you stay up?

_____ **8.** When does he visit you?

a. Till 10:00 or 11:00.

b. I go home.

c. On Sundays.

~~**d.**~~ At about 6:00 A.M.

e. My parents and my brother.

f. She's my cousin.

g. On Main Street.

h. I don't have a car.

2 | WH- QUESTIONS WITH THE SIMPLE PRESENT

Read the statements. Complete the questions. Use the simple present.

1. A: I go to school.

   B: Where _____ *do you go to school?* _____

2. A: I don't go to school alone.

   B: Who _____ with you?

3. A: I don't get to school by bus.

   B: How _____

4. A: We have nice conversations.

   B: What _____

5. A: My brother goes to school early.

   B: Why _____

(continued)

6. A: Ms. Thomas gets home late.

  B: What time _____

7. A: We like to play tennis.

  B: When _____

3 | TELLING TIME

Look at the examples. Write the times.

It's seven o'clock.
It's seven.

It's five after seven.

It's a quarter after
  seven.
It's seven-fifteen.

It's half past seven.
It's seven-thirty.

It's seven thirty-five.
It's twenty-five to
  eight.

It's a quarter to eight.
It's seven forty-five.

1. 7:40 *It's seven-forty.* OR *It's twenty to eight.* _____

2. 7:10 _____

3. 3:02 _____

4. 4:40 _____

5. 8:50 _____

6. 7:55 _____

7. 11:00 _____

   8. 1:30 _____

   9. 2:15 _____

 10. 6:45 _____

 11. 10:25 _____

 12. 3:35 _____

4 | *WH-* QUESTIONS WITH THE SIMPLE PRESENT

Write questions about the underlined expressions. Use **what**, **what time**, **where**, **who**, *or* **why**.

 1. **A:** _What time do you wake up?_ _____

     B: I wake up <u>at 7:30</u>.

 2. **A:** _____

     B: My mother? <u>She's an engineer.</u>

 3. **A:** _____

     B: <u>Because</u> I like jazz. It's my favorite music.

 4. **A:** _____

     B: Dinner? Usually <u>at 6:00</u>.

 5. **A:** _____

     B: <u>Because</u> he starts work at 5:00 A.M.

 6. **A:** _____

     B: Two of my cousins live <u>in New York</u>. My other cousins live <u>in different cities</u>.

 7. **A:** _____

     B: <u>My uncle</u> owns the restaurant.

5 | EDITING

Correct the conversation. There are eight mistakes. The first two mistakes are already corrected.

                 does   *start*

YUKO: What time ^English class ~~starts~~?

OMAR: At 1:00.

YUKO: What time class finish?

(continued)

OMAR: At 2:30.

YUKO: What means *dislike*?

OMAR: It means "not like."

YUKO: How you say this word?

OMAR: I don't know.

YUKO: Do the teacher teach every day?

OMAR: No. She doesn't teach on Friday.

YUKO: What have we for homework?

OMAR: Page 97.

YUKO: Why does Elena know all the answers?

OMAR: She study a lot.

6 | CONVERSATION COMPLETION

Complete the conversation. Use the words in the box. Don't look at your Student Book.

does	~~how do you like~~	let's go	sleep in	time	Why
else	late	off	till	What	work

JEREMY: So . . . _____how do you like_____ the United States?
                              1.

YOSHIO: I like it a lot. But it's really different from Japan.

JEREMY: _____ do you mean?
                    2.

YOSHIO: Well, for one thing, I think people _____ longer hours in Japan.
                                                        3.

JEREMY: Some people work pretty _____ here too. What time do people go to bed
                                               4.
there?

YOSHIO: Well, students study a lot, so they stay up till midnight or later. And my father stays up

_____ 1:00 or 2:00 A.M.
        5.

JEREMY: _____ does he stay up so late? What does he do?
              6.

YOSHIO: He's a businessman. People in business often meet clients in the evening.

JEREMY: What _____ do people get up in the morning in Japan?
                    7.

YOSHIO: Oh, maybe seven or seven-thirty. I _____ on weekends.
                                                      8.

JEREMY: Me too. Hmm . . . What _____ is different?
                                         9.

YOSHIO: Hmm . . . Well, people wear their shoes in the house here. In Japan we take our shoes

_____ at the doorway.
        10.

JEREMY: Really? Everyone?

YOSHIO: Yes, everyone.

JEREMY: So what do you like best about the United States?

YOSHIO: People here are really open, and I have a lot of friends at Redmond High School.

JEREMY: That's great. Hey, we have to go to calculus class.

YOSHIO: What time _____ it start?
                          11.

JEREMY: Two-thirty.

YOSHIO: OK, _____.
                  12.

12 The Simple Present: *Be* and *Have*

1 | SIMPLE PRESENT STATEMENTS WITH *BE* AND *HAVE*

Look at the pictures. Complete the sentences. Use **is**, **isn't**, **are**, **aren't**, **has**, **doesn't have**, **have**, *or* **don't have**.

Mike   **Susan**   **Peter**   **Cheryl**

Ben   **Liam**   **Jen**   **Holly**

1. Holly _____*is*_____ heavy. She _*doesn't have*_ dark hair.

2. Liam _____ short. He _____ curly hair.

3. Susan and Cheryl _____ tall. They _____ curly dark hair.

4. Mike _____ tall. He _____ straight blond hair.

5. Ben and Cheryl _____ thin. They _____ blond hair.

6. Susan _____ pregnant. She _____ straight blond hair.

7. Peter _____ heavy. He _____ straight dark hair.

8. Jen _____ pregnant. She _____ straight dark hair.

2 | SIMPLE PRESENT STATEMENTS WITH *BE* AND *HAVE*

Complete the sentences about yourself. Use **'m**, **'m not**, **have**, *or* **don't have**.

1. I <u> 'm OR 'm not </u> divorced.

2. I _____ one brother and

    one sister.

3. I _____ 19 years old.

4. I _____ hazel eyes.

5. I _____ curly hair.

6. I _____ a university

    student.

7. I _____ a job.

8. I _____ tall.

9. I _____ from Mexico.

10. I _____ light brown hair.

3 | SIMPLE PRESENT STATEMENTS WITH *BE* AND *HAVE*

Complete the description. Use the correct forms of **be** *or* **have**.

These _____<u>are</u>_____ pictures of Bono and his band. The name of the band _____
    1.   **2.**

U2. Bono _____ the singer in the band.
            3.

    Bono _____ the singer's real name. His real name _____ Paul Hewson. He
            4.   **5.**

_____ from Dublin, Ireland. He _____ one brother, but he _____ any
   6.   **7.**   **8.**

sisters.

    Bono _____ married to Alison Stewart. They _____ four children—two
            9.   **10.**

daughters and two sons. They _____ a home in Dublin. Their children's names
                                11.

_____ Jordan, Memphis Eve, Elijah, and John Abraham.
   12.

4 | SIMPLE PRESENT QUESTIONS WITH *BE* AND *HAVE*

*Write questions about Bono. Use the words in parentheses and the correct forms of **be**
or **have**. Use **do** or **does** where needed.*

1. (Who / the man in the pictures / ?) *Who's the man in the pictures?*

2. (Bono / in a band / ?) *Is Bono in a band?*

3. (What / the name of Bono's band / ?) _____

4. (Bono / a violinist / ?) _____

5. (What / Bono's real name / ?) _____

6. (Where / he from / ?) _____

7. (he / any brothers or sisters / ?) _____

8. (he / married / ?) _____

9. (they / children / ?) _____

10. (Where / they / a home / ?) _____

5 | EDITING

Correct the conversation. There are eight mistakes. The first mistake is already corrected.

      What's
A: ~~What~~ your name?

B: Alice.

A: How old have you?

B: I have 24.

A: You have a big family?

B: Yes, I do. I have three sisters and four brothers.

A: Where do you live?

B: My home near here. It's on Center Street.

A: Is big?

B: No. It small. I live alone. My family lives in another city.

A: Have you a job?

B: No. I study at a university.

6 | CONVERSATION COMPLETION

Complete the conversation. Use the words in the box. Don't look at your Student Book.

are	has	in	pregnant	She's	unusual
doesn't	heads	look like	right away	these	~~you~~

RICK: You're in Music Appreciation 101, aren't

_____*you*_____?
1.

JUDY: Uh-huh . . .

RICK: Could you please give _____ tickets to
2.

Sonia Jones? She's in your music appreciation class.

JUDY: Sure. But I don't know her. What does she

_____?
3.

RICK: Well, she _____ dark hair and dark
4.

eyes.

JUDY: Half the women have dark hair and dark eyes. And

there _____ 100 students in my class.
5.

RICK: _____ tall and thin.
6.

JUDY: OK, but a lot of women are tall and thin.

RICK: She's _____ her early twenties.
7.

JUDY: Rick. That _____ help. Almost
8.

everyone at school is 20-something. Is there

something _____ about her?
9.

RICK: She has two _____.
10.

JUDY: Rick!

RICK: Sonia's eight months _____. And her
11.

cell phone number is 917-555-0934.

JUDY: Why didn't you say so _____?
12.

RICK: It's more fun this way.

13 Adverbs of Frequency

1 | ADVERBS OF FREQUENCY WITH *BE* AND OTHER VERBS

Complete the sentences so they are true. Use **always**, **usually**, **often**, **sometimes**, **rarely**, *or* **never**.

1. I _____ wake up on time.

2. I _____ get up early.

3. I _____ go to bed very late.

4. I'm _____ tired in the afternoon.

5. I _____ have fun on the weekend.

6. I'm _____ hungry in the morning.

7. I _____ exercise in the morning.

8. I _____ eat dinner alone.

2 | WORD ORDER WITH ADVERBS OF FREQUENCY

Put the words in the correct order. Write sentences. Don't change any capitalization.

1. late / sleep / never / I / .   *I never sleep late.* _____

2. does / Steve / exercise / often / not / . _____

3. rarely / a / Bill / restaurant / eats / at / . _____

4. here / It / snows / sometimes / . _____

5. Mary / not / usually / busy / is / . _____

6. Cairo / often / is / It / hot / in / . _____

3 | ADVERBS OF FREQUENCY

Rewrite the sentences. Replace the underlined words. Use **always**, **often**, **sometimes**, **rarely**, *or* **never**.

1. I drink coffee <u>every day</u>.   *I always drink coffee.*

2. I play soccer <u>one or two times a month</u>. _____

3. I am late for class <u>one or two times a year</u>. _____

4. The food at that restaurant is <u>not</u> good. _____

5. Jennifer sees a play <u>one time a year</u>. _____

6. Robert goes to the movies <u>two times a week</u>. _____

4 | ADVERBS OF FREQUENCY

Look at the picture. Write a sentence about each person. Use **always**, **usually**, **sometimes**, *or* **never** *and the words in parentheses.*

S ☐   M ☑   T ☑   W ☑   Th ☑   F ☑   S ☐

Jackson

1.   *Jackson is always on time for school.*
            (be on time for school)

S ☐   M ☐   T ☐   W ☐   Th ☐   F ☐   S ☐

Robert

2. _____
     (cook)

(continued)

Nick

S ☐ M ☑ T ☑ W ☑ Th ☑ F ☑ S ☑

3. _____
(go to the gym)

Mr. and Mrs. Lee

S ☐ M ☐ T ☐ W ☐ Th ☐ F ☐ S ☑

4. _____
(go to a restaurant)

Ruth

S ☑ M ☑ T ☑ W ☑ Th ☑ F ☑ S ☑

5. _____
(eat lunch)

5 | QUESTIONS WITH *EVER* AND *HOW OFTEN*

Write a question for each answer. Use **ever** *or* **how often**.

1. **A:** _How often do you go dancing?_ _____

   B: Go dancing? I never go dancing.

2. **A:** _____

   B: Yes, I do. I go to the theater two or three times a year.

3. A: _____

B: No, they don't. My children never stay home alone.

4. A: _____

B: The radio? I listen to the radio every day.

5. A: _____

B: No, never. I never smoke.

6. A: _____

B: Tim? He cooks dinner one or two times a week.

7. A: _____

B: Yes. I'm usually home on the weekend.

---

6 | EDITING

Correct the e-mail. There are six mistakes. The first mistake is already corrected.

Subj: My schedule
Date: Friday, September 15
From: BJones@AU.edu
To: SamD92@AU.edu

Hi, Sam,

                               am usually

    Here is my schedule. I ~~usually am~~ busy on Monday evenings. I go often to the gym, or I play basketball. (Do ever you play basketball?) On Fridays always I exercise too. I go dancing at the club! On Wednesdays and Thursdays I sometimes work late, but I'm often free on Tuesdays. I finish work usually at 5:30. Do you want to meet at Vincenzo's Italian Restaurant at 6:30 on Tuesday? The food there is good always.

Bob

7 | CONVERSATION COMPLETION

Complete the conversation. Use the words in the box. Don't look at your Student Book.

about	breakfast	~~going~~	kind of	sleep	times
always	ever	hurry	often	Sometimes	usually

JOSH: How's it _____*going*_____, Steve? You look
1.

_____ tired.
2.

STEVE: Things are fine. I *am* a little tired, though.

JOSH: That's too bad. Any idea why?

STEVE: Well, I don't know . . . Maybe I'm not getting

enough _____.
3.

JOSH: How many hours do you get a night?

STEVE: Oh, _____ six.
4.

JOSH: What time do you _____ go to bed?
5.

STEVE: I usually stay up till 12:30 or 1:00. And I get up at 6:30 or 7:00. On weekdays, anyway.

JOSH: Do you _____ sleep late?
6.

STEVE: _____—on the weekend.
7.

JOSH: And you always have fast food for lunch. And sometimes it's junk food.

STEVE: Well . . . yes . . . and I sometimes skip _____.
8.

JOSH: So you don't eat three meals a day? Breakfast, lunch, and dinner?

STEVE: Well . . . not really. I'm usually in a _____ in the morning. So I skip breakfast.
9.

JOSH: No good, my friend. What about lunch and dinner?

STEVE: I always have a good dinner. But lunch . . . well, I usually go to a fast-food place near the

university. I'm _____ in a hurry.
10.

JOSH: Hmm. Not enough sleep. No breakfast. Junk food for lunch sometimes. You're living

dangerously.

STEVE: Maybe. But I have one good habit. I exercise.

JOSH: Great. How _____?
11.

STEVE: Two or three _____ a year.
12.

The Present Progressive: Statements

1 | AFFIRMATIVE STATEMENTS WITH THE PRESENT PROGRESSIVE

Match the sentences.

__e__ 1. Mary is at the library.

_____ 2. The little boy is in his bedroom.

_____ 3. My father's in the kitchen.

_____ 4. Mark and Amanda are at a restaurant.

_____ 5. Judy's in her office.

_____ 6. The students are in the classroom.

_____ 7. The boys are at the park.

_____ 8. My grandmother's in the hospital.

a. They're playing soccer.

b. She's talking to her doctor.

c. They're writing sentences.

d. He's sleeping.

e. She's reading a book.

f. He's cooking.

g. They're eating.

h. She's working at her computer.

2 | BASE FORM AND VERB + -ING

*Write the **-ing** form of the verbs.*

Base Form	Base Form + *-ing*	Base Form	Base Form + *-ing*
1. ask	_____asking_____	7. look	_____
2. close	_____	8. listen	_____
3. do	_____	9. move	_____
4. stop	_____	10. open	_____
5. enjoy	_____	11. run	_____
6. fix	_____	12. try	_____

3 | AFFIRMATIVE STATEMENTS WITH THE PRESENT PROGRESSIVE

Look at the picture. Complete the paragraph. Use the verbs in the box and the present progressive.

answer	cook	help	listen	~~play~~	read	wash	work

Things are happening at the Olson house today. Annie and Ben _____*are playing*_____ video
                                                                    1.
games. Jeremy and his friend _____ to music and _____ magazines.
                                        2.   **3.**
Grandma _____ dinner. Grandpa _____ the dishes, and Tim
                4.   **5.**
_____ Grandpa. Jessica _____ at the computer. She
        6.   **7.**
_____ her e-mail.
        8.

4 | AFFIRMATIVE AND NEGATIVE STATEMENTS WITH THE PRESENT PROGRESSIVE

Write true sentences about yourself. Use the words in parentheses and the present progressive.

1. (I / wear / a jacket / right now)

   I'm wearing a jacket right now. OR *I'm not wearing a jacket right now.*

2. (I / wear / glasses / right now)

   _____

3. (I / listen / to music / right now)

_____

4. (I / sit / in my bedroom / right now)

_____

5. (I / eat / right now)

_____

6. (I / sit / with my friend / right now)

_____

7. (I / drink / water / right now)

_____

8. (I / look / at a computer / right now)

_____

5 | EDITING

Correct the postcard. There are eight mistakes. The first mistake is already corrected.

                    It's

Hello from Seattle. ~~It~~ raining right now, but we have fun. Jenny and I are sit in a restaurant. I eating lunch. The food here in Seattle is good. Jenny no is eating. She drink coffee. We aren't talk. Jenny's read the newspaper. I hope you're fine.

            Love,

            Amy

Mom and Dad
40 McPherson St.
Allawah NSW 2218
Australia

6 | CONVERSATION COMPLETION

Complete the conversation. Use the words in the box. Don't look at your Student Book.

Come on over	~~going on~~	isn't studying	looking	See you soon	waiting
computer	is	lasagna	'm	studying	watching

JEREMY: Hello.

DANNY: Hey, Jeremy? This is Danny.

JEREMY: Hi, Danny. Where are you? What's

_____*going on*_____? Are you with Hiro and Ron?
     1.

DANNY: No. Hiro's _____.
             2.

JEREMY: Don't tell me Ron's studying too.

DANNY: No. Ron _____. He's working. I'm with Matt. We're at the video store on
        3.

Jackson Avenue. We're _____ at the new games. Why don't you come
          4.

over?

JEREMY: I can't. I _____ watching my sister and brother.
        5.

DANNY: Bring them along.

JEREMY: Impossible. They're _____ videos and
          6.

_____ for my Uncle Steve. Today's Ben's
     7.

birthday, and Uncle Steve has some

_____ games for him.
     8.

DANNY: Cool. Maybe Ben wants some help.

JEREMY: Sure. _____. My grandma is making
        9.

vegetable soup and _____ and my
         10.

grandpa _____ baking a cake. Stay for
       11.

dinner.

DANNY: Thanks. We can play games all night.

JEREMY: Great. _____.
       12.

The Present Progressive: Yes / No Questions

1 | SHORT ANSWERS WITH THE PRESENT PROGRESSIVE

Answer the questions. Write true short answers.

1. Are you listening to music? *Yes, I am.* OR *No, I'm not.* _____

2. Is it raining? _____

3. Is the sun shining? _____

4. Are you doing your homework? _____

5. Are your friends doing their homework with you? _____

6. Are you having fun? _____

7. Are you working hard? _____

8. Are you eating a snack? _____

2 | *YES / NO* QUESTIONS AND SHORT ANSWERS WITH THE PRESENT PROGRESSIVE

Write questions in the present progressive. Then complete the short answers. Use the information in parentheses.

1. **A:** *Is she writing a letter?* _____

   B: Yes, *she is.* _____ (She's writing a letter.)

2. **A:** _____

   B: No, _____ (He's not sleeping in his bedroom.)

3. **A:** _____

   B: Yes, _____ (The Smiths are eating dinner.)

4. **A:** _____

   B: No, _____ (Ben isn't doing his homework.)

(continued)

5. A: _____

    B: No, _____ (The children aren't cleaning the kitchen.)

6. A: _____

    B: Yes, _____ (Paula's drinking coffee with milk.)

3 | YES / NO QUESTIONS AND SHORT ANSWERS WITH THE PRESENT PROGRESSIVE

Look at the picture. Write questions. Use the words in parentheses and the present progressive. Then write short answers.

1. (Jessica and Tim / eat at a restaurant)

    Are Jessica and Tim eating at a restaurant?   *No, they aren't.*

2. (Jessica / wear a hat)

    Is Jessica wearing a hat?   *No, she isn't.*

3. (Jessica / cook dinner)

    _____   _____

4. (the cat / wear a hat)

    _____   _____

5. (Ben and Annie / play cards)

    _____   _____

6. (Jeremy / listen to music)

    _____   _____

7. (Tim / write a letter)

   _____   _____

8. (the cat / sit on the floor)

   _____   _____

9. (the cat / read)

   _____   _____

4 | STATEMENTS AND *YES / NO* QUESTIONS WITH THE PRESENT PROGRESSIVE

Complete the conversation. Write statements and yes / no *questions in the present progressive. Use the words in parentheses.*

GAIL: _____*Is your mother baking*_____ ?
　　　　　　　　1. (your mother / bake)

ANNIE: No, that's my brother. _____ cookies.
　　　　　　　　　　　　　　　　　2. (he / make)

GAIL: _____ in the dining room?
　　　　　3. (your parents / eat)

ANNIE: No, that's Kelly, the babysitter. _____ dinner at a restaurant.
　　　　　　　　　　　　　　　　　　　　4. (my parents / have)

　　　　It's their anniversary.

GAIL: What about Jeremy? _____ ?
　　　　　　　　　　　　　　5. (he / sleep)

ANNIE: No, he isn't. _____ a baseball game with our uncle.
　　　　　　　　　6. (he / watch)

5 | EDITING

Correct the conversations. There are ten mistakes. The first mistake is already corrected.

1. **A:** Are you ~~sleep~~? *(sleeping)*

   B: No, I not.

2. **A:** The teacher giving us homework?

   B: Yes, she's.

3. **A:** Is Mr. Olson work?

   B: No, he isn't. He's eat lunch.

4. **A:** Is sleeping Kelly?

   B: No, she's not. She watching a DVD with her friend.

5. **A:** Is Tim and his boss wearing suits?

   B: Yes, they're.

6 | CONVERSATION COMPLETION

Complete the conversations. Use the words in the box. Don't look at your Student Book.

babysitting	be back	cool	Everything's	~~Is~~	studying
baking	check	everything	helping	listening	watching

TIM: Hi, hon. Happy Anniversary!

JESSICA: Thanks. You too.

TIM: Everyone OK at home? _____Is_____ Jeremy
1.
_____ Ben and Annie?
2.

JESSICA: No. Jeremy's at a ball game with Steve.

TIM: Oh. Is Mrs. Brody _____?
3.

JESSICA: No. Kelly Brown is. You know her.

[Later—Jessica calls Kelly.]

KELLY: Hello?

JESSICA: Hi, Kelly. This is Mrs. Olson. How's _____?
4.
Are the children _____ to you?
5.

KELLY: Sure. _____ great.
6.

JESSICA: So are you _____ Ben with his math?
7.

KELLY: No, not now. He's _____ cookies. He's a
8.
really sweet kid.

JESSICA: Thanks. Is Annie _____ for her science test?
9.

KELLY: I think so. Her friend Gail is here. They're in Annie's room.

It's quiet. They're probably studying.

JESSICA: Hmm. Well, I'm sure they are. Can you

_____?
10.

KELLY: OK, Mrs. Olson. Look. Don't worry. Everything's

_____. Enjoy your anniversary.
11.

JESSICA: Thanks, Kelly. We'll _____ around 11:00.
12.

KELLY: Bye.

The Present Progressive: *Wh-* Questions

1 | QUESTION WORDS

Write the correct question words. Use **Who, What, Where, Why,** *or* **How.**

1. ___*Where*___ ? On the grass by the pond.

2. _____ ? Jeremy.

3. _____ ? Listening to music.

4. _____ ? On a blanket.

5. _____ ? Because they're hungry.

6. _____ ? Happy.

7. _____ ? They're riding bikes.

8. _____ ? On a bench.

9. _____ ? Bill is.

10. _____ ? They're swimming.

2 | *WH-* QUESTIONS AND ANSWERS WITH THE PRESENT PROGRESSIVE

Write questions. Use the words in parentheses and the present progressive. Then find an answer in Exercise 1 for each question.

1. (Who / read / a book / ?)

   Who is reading a book?   *Bill is.*

2. (Why / Jessica and Tim / eat / ?)

   _____   _____

3. (What / the ducks / do / ?)

   _____   _____

4. (Where / Mary and Bill / sit / ?)

   _____   _____

5. (How / everyone / feel / ?)

   _____   _____

6. (Where / Jeremy / sit / ?)

   _____   _____

7. (Who / listen to / music / ?)

   _____   _____

8. (What / Annie and Ben / do ?)

   _____   _____

3 | *WH-* QUESTIONS WITH THE PRESENT PROGRESSIVE

*Complete the conversations. Write questions with **where**, **what**, **why**, or **who**.*

1. **A:** I'm sitting in the garden.

   B: _____ *Why are you sitting* _____ there?

   A: It's a beautiful day.

2. **A:** Shh! I'm talking.

   B: _____ to?

   A: My grandfather.

3. **A:** The children are baking.

   B: _____?

   A: Cookies.

4. **A:** Mrs. Brody isn't watching Ben and Annie.

   B: _____ the kids?

   A: Her granddaughter Kelly is.

5. **A:** Jeremy's studying.

   B: _____?

   A: At the library.

4 | EDITING

Correct the conversations. There are eight mistakes. The first mistake is already corrected.

1. **A:** What ~~you are~~ doing?
   _{are you}

   B: My homework.

2. **A:** What the people watching?

   B: The soccer game.

3. **A:** Why Mark is wearing a suit?

   B: Because he going to a wedding.

4. **A:** What's everything going?

   B: Great. We are have a lot of fun.

5. **A:** Where Ben and Annie are going?

   B: To their grandmother's house.

6. **A:** Who's Jeremy send an e-mail message to?

   B: A friend from school.

5 | CONVERSATION COMPLETION

Complete the conversations. Use the words in the box. Don't look at your Student Book.

~~Dad's~~	I'm	out	What	Where's	Why
Fish stew	on	starved	What's	Who	why don't

ANNIE: Hey, Mom. _____Dad's_____ driving down the
1.

street. _____ he going?
2.

JESSICA: To the store.

ANNIE: _____ is he going to the store now?
3.

JESSICA: We're _____ of milk.
4.

ANNIE: Oh. _____ for dinner?
5.

JESSICA: Your favorite!

ANNIE: My favorite? Really? What?

JESSICA: _____.
6.

ANNIE: Mom! Come _____! Are you kidding?
7.

JESSICA: Yes, _____ kidding.
8.

[Later]

JEREMY: Hi, Mom. _____ are you talking to?
9.

JESSICA: Dad. He's at the supermarket.

JEREMY: Oh. _____ are you making?
10.

JESSICA: Tacos and beans.

JEREMY: Mmm. Super. I'm _____. Mom, this is
11.

my friend Yoshio.

JESSICA: It's nice to meet you, Yoshio. Can you stay for dinner?

YOSHIO: It's nice to meet you too. Yes, I would love to stay for

dinner. Thank you.

JESSICA: Wonderful. Now, Jeremy, _____ you go and help Ben? He's writing a
12.

report for school. He needs help on the computer.

JEREMY: Oh, all right. These kids!

Possessive Nouns;
This / That / These / Those

1 | *THIS / THAT / THESE / THOSE*

What are the people saying? Complete the conversations. Write questions with **what** *and* **this**, **that**, **these**, *or* **those**.

1. **A:** _____*What are these?*_____

   B: _____*Those*_____ are maracas.

2. **A:** _____

   B: _____ are alpacas.

3. **A:** _____

   B: I don't know!

4. **A:** _____

   B: _____ a skunk!

2 | VOCABULARY AND POSSESSIVE NOUNS

Look at the picture. Complete the sentences. Use possessive nouns.

1. _____Josh's_____ cell phone is working.

2. _____ sports jacket looks sharp.

3. _____ pants are black. She's wearing them with a black jacket.

4. _____ skirt is not long.

5. _____ tie is new.

Josh   Diego   Gabrielle   Pam

3 | POSSESSIVE NOUNS

*Correct the sentences. Add '**s** or ' where necessary. The first sentence is already corrected.*

1. Jessica house is big.   (with 's inserted: Jessica's house is big.)

2. His parents names are Jessica and Tim.

3. Steve apartment is in Seattle.

4. The students tests are on the desk.

5. The teacher book is in her bag.

6. Our daughters husbands are very nice.

7. The children room is on the second floor.

8. My friend grandchildren visit her every weekend.

4 | POSSESSIVE 'S OR CONTRACTION?

Rewrite the sentences where possible. Replace contractions with full forms.

1. Jack's wearing black shoes. _Jack is wearing black shoes._

2. Who's wearing Mara's jacket? _____

3. That's not Sam's house. _____

4. The baby's not sleeping. _____

5. Steve's last name is Jones. _____

6. Amanda's here. _____

7. It's Jessica's car. _____

5 | EDITING

Correct the conversations. There are six mistakes. The first mistake is already corrected.

                        mother's
1. **A:** Does my ~~mother~~ jacket look good on me?

   B: Hmm. I'm not sure.

2. **A:** The women restroom is over there.

   B: Thanks.

3. **A:** Who's this over there?

   B: That's Ken.

4. **A:** Does Ken usually wear ties?

   B: No. He's wearing his brother tie. And this isn't Ken's sports jacket either.

5. **A:** Those earrings look really good on Judy.

   B: Yeah. I like these earrings too.

6 | CONVERSATION COMPLETION

Complete the conversation. Use the words in the box. Don't look at your Student Book.

brother's	love	~~occasion~~	parents'	that	those
Kathy's	No kidding	parents	roomates	these	yours

MARK: Judy, do I look OK?

JUDY: Yeah. You look really sharp. What's the

_____occasion_____?
1.

MARK: I'm having dinner with Kathy and her

_____. It's her _____
2.   **3.**

anniversary. They're taking us to The Water Grill.

JUDY: That's terrific. Is that a new jacket?

MARK: It's my _____ jacket.
4.

JUDY: It's nice.

MARK: Are _____ suspenders OK?
5.

JUDY: Sure. They go well with that tie and

_____ shoes.
6.

MARK: Thanks. Actually they aren't mine. They're my

_____.
7.

JUDY: Oh yeah? Is *anything* _____?
8.

MARK: Uh-huh. This new goatee. It's all mine.

JUDY: Oh. I see. You know, _____ goatee makes
9.

you look like a doctor.

MARK: A doctor? _____. I guess that's good.
10.

Now I need to remember—_____ mom is
11.

Bea Harlow, and her dad is Lee White.

JUDY: Relax, Mark. They're going to _____
12.

you!

Count and Non-count Nouns; *Some* and *Any*

1 | COUNT AND NON-COUNT NOUNS

Write **a**, **an**, *or* **some** *before each word.*

1. ___*a*___ bagel

2. _____ banana

3. _____ bread

4. _____ cereal

5. _____ chip

6. _____ coffee

7. _____ egg

8. _____ fruit

9. _____ hamburger

10. _____ ice cream

11. _____ juice

12. _____ milk

13. _____ olive

14. _____ orange

15. _____ peach

16. _____ peanut butter

17. _____ rice

18. _____ sandwich

19. _____ soda

20. _____ spaghetti

21. _____ strawberry

22. _____ toast

23. _____ water

24. _____ yogurt

2 | SOME AND ANY

Complete the sentences. Use **some** *or* **any**.

1. I don't have _____*any*_____ money.

2. I don't want _____ cereal.

3. Do they have _____ peanut butter?

4. Julie needs _____ coffee.

5. Does he want _____ juice?

6. We want _____ sandwiches.

7. Steve has _____ eggs and a slice of toast.

8. Do you have _____ strawberries?

3 | QUANTIFIERS WITH NON-COUNT NOUNS

Complete the sentences. Cross out the incorrect word in parentheses.

1. Would you like a (bottle / ~~slice~~ / glass) of water?

2. I have a (bowl / bottle / glass) of iced tea.

3. Here is (some / a bottle of / a cup of) coffee for you.

4. Please get me a (slice / piece / cup) of bread.

5. Do you want (some / a glass of / a bowl of) ice cream?

4 | VERB AGREEMENT WITH COUNT AND NON-COUNT NOUNS

*Write statements or questions. Use the words in parentheses and **is** or **are**. Remember to add the correct capitalization.*

1. (apples / any / there / ?)

   Are there any apples?

2. (good / you / fruit / for / .)

   _____

3. (eggs / any / for breakfast / there / ?)

   _____

4. (delicious / the / ice cream / .)

   _____

5. (the / at that restaurant / good / food / ?)

   _____

6. (some / bread / there / .)

   _____

7. (any / milk / there / ?)

   _____

8. (salty / olives / these / .)

   _____

5 | COUNT AND NON-COUNT NOUNS

Complete the sentences. Use **a**, **an**, **any**, *or* **some**.

1. I don't have _____*any*_____ sisters or brothers.

2. I'm writing _____*an*_____ e-mail message.

3. Do you have _____ questions?

4. I have _____ question.

5. I need _____ answer to this question.

6. I know _____ people from Canada.

7. I don't have _____ American friends.

8. We have _____ apartment on Main Street.

9. Is that _____ good restaurant?

10. We want _____ tea.

11. I don't want _____ ice cream.

12. Please give me _____ bananas.

6 | EDITING

Correct the conversation. There are seven mistakes. The first mistake is already corrected.

Judy: Excuse me, waiter? Hi. Can I have ~~some~~ *a* glass of water, please?

Waiter: Sure. Ma'am, do you want mineral or regular?

Judy: Regular, please.

[Minutes later]

Waiter: Here is your water. Are you ready to order?

Judy: Yes. I'd like sandwich and a bowl of soup. Oh, and some small piece of chocolate cake too.

Waiter: And you, sir?

Josh: Well, I'm not sure. Are the spaghetti here good?

Waiter: Yes, it's delicious.

Josh: OK. I'd like any spaghetti. And bowl of ice cream.

Waiter: And what about something to drink?

Josh: I want the water. Mineral water, please.

7 | CONVERSATION COMPLETION

Complete the conversations. Use the words in the box. Don't look at your Student Book.

~~all~~	an	at	cup	glass	some
	any	bowl	fruit	on	strawberries

JESSICA: Hello, everyone. This morning we're interviewing people about their eating habits . . . Excuse me, sir, do you eat breakfast?

MAN: Yes, I do.

JESSICA: What do you have?

MAN: I have _____*a*_____ bagel and a _____ of
1.   2.
coffee.

JESSICA: That's _____? Do you have _____
3.   4.
juice or anything else to drink?

MAN: Nope. That's all—just a bagel and coffee. I'm always in a hurry. Bye.

JESSICA: OK. Thanks. Bye.

JESSICA: Now, here's our next person. Ma'am, what do you have for breakfast?

WOMAN 1: I never eat breakfast.

JESSICA: Nothing _____ all?
5.

WOMAN 1: No. I'm _____ a diet. I'm *always* on a diet.
6.

JESSICA: OK. Thank you . . .

JESSICA: And what about you, ma'am? What do you have for breakfast?

WOMAN 2: Oh, I usually have a _____ of cereal and
7.
_____ yogurt with _____—a banana,
8.   9.
a peach or _____ orange, or some
10.
_____. And I have a _____ of juice.
11.   12.

JESSICA: Hmm. That sounds healthy.

WOMAN 2: Yes, I always eat a good breakfast.

JESSICA: All right, thanks. Let's see what our next person says . . .

19   *A / An* and *The*; *One / Ones*

1 | *ONE / ONES*

Match the statements and questions with the responses.

__f__ 1. I like the blue umbrella.

____ 2. Here are your new suspenders.

____ 3. Do you like the stores on Main Street?

____ 4. I like the black pants.

____ 5. This is your new office.

____ 6. Do you go to the Italian restaurant
on Park Street?

a. No, I don't like that one.

b. No, I like the ones on First
Street.

c. I like the brown ones.

d. I like the old one.

e. I want the old ones.

f. Really? I like the red one.

2 | *ONE / ONES*

*Look at the pictures. Answer the questions. Use **one** or **ones**.*

1. Do you like the old car or the new car?

I like the _____*old one* OR *new one*_____.

2. Do you like the formal clothes or the casual clothes?

I like the _____.

3. Do you like the expensive earrings or the cheap earrings?

I like the _____.

4. Do you like the big car or the small car?

I like the _____.

5. Do you like the bright sweater or the dull sweater?

I like the _____.

3 | A / AN AND *THE*

Look at the picture. Complete the conversation. Use **a**, **an**, *or* **the**.

A: What's in the picture?

B: I see _____*an*_____ apartment. I see _____ boy and _____ girl.
         1.   **2.**   **3.**

A: Where is _____ boy?
               4.

B: He's sitting on _____ chair.
                    5.

A: Where is _____ girl?
               6.

B: _____ girl is next to _____ window.
   7.   **8.**

A: What is she doing?

B: She's watching _____ sun come up.
                   9.

A: What is _____ boy doing?
             10.

B: He's eating _____ apple.
                11.

4 | ARTICLE OR NO ARTICLE?

Complete the paragraphs. Use **a**, **an**, *or* **the**. *If no article is needed, write* **Ø**.

I shop at Clothes for You. It's _____*a*_____ nice store. It always has _____*Ø*_____ clothes in my
                                    1.   **2.**

size. It has _____ clothes for _____ men and _____ women. _____ clothes there
          3.   **4.**   **5.**   **6.**

are always nice and not very expensive.

I go to Nice Feet for _____ shoes. _____ shoes there are a little expensive, but they're
                           7.   **8.**

always comfortable. It's _____ big store, and it's usually busy. I know _____ clerk there. I
                         9.   **10.**

don't know his name, but he's the only clerk there with _____ goatee. He also always wears
                                                  11.

_____ orange tie.
12.

5 | EDITING

Correct the conversations. There are eight mistakes. The first mistake is already corrected.

1. **A:** Try on the green jacket.

   B: But I prefer the brown. ^one^

2. **A:** What's your favorite food?

   B: I like the Chinese food.

3. **A:** Do you wear your black slacks to school?

   B: No, I usually wear my gray one.

4. **A:** Do you wear the tie to work?

   B: No, I don't like the ties.

5. **A:** Do you have an white dress that I could try on?

   B: Yes, I do. Here's a small one and here's a large one.

6. **A:** Do you want a umbrella?

   B: No, I never use the umbrellas.

6 | CONVERSATION COMPLETION

Complete the conversation. Use the words in the box. Don't look at your Student Book.

a	in	~~May~~	one	sale	the
an	look	on	ones	size	up

CLERK: _____May_____ I help you?
                1.

KEN: Yes, I'm looking for _____ new sports
                                        2.

jacket. I have _____ interview tomorrow.
                      3.

CLERK: Oh, you're _____ luck! We're having a
                              4.

_____ on sports jackets.
        5.

KEN: You are? Great!

CLERK: What _____?
                      6.

KEN: Forty-two.

CLERK: OK. Be right back.

(continued)

CLERK: All right. Do you like any of these?

KEN: Yes! I really like _____ blue one.
7.

CLERK: Do you want to try it _____?
8.

KEN: Sure.

CLERK: How does it feel?

KEN: Really comfortable. How does it _____,
9.

Laura?

LAURA: Well, it's pretty bright. And it's casual. How about

that black _____? It's more formal.
10.

KEN: All the black _____ are dull—really
11.

boring.

LAURA: OK. It's _____ to you.
12.

Can / Can't

1 | AFFIRMATIVE AND NEGATIVE STATEMENTS WITH *CAN*

Complete the sentences. Use **can** *or* **can't**.

1. A bird _____*can*_____ fly.

2. A dog _____ fly.

3. A new baby _____ talk.

4. A fish _____ swim.

5. A cat _____ climb trees.

6. An elephant _____ climb trees.

(continued)

7. A child _____ drive a car.

8. A bird _____ sing.

2 | YES / NO QUESTIONS WITH CAN

Rewrite the requests. Use **can**.

1. Please do me a favor. _Can you do me a favor, please?_ _____

2. Give Kathy this message, please. _____

3. Tell me the answers, please. _____

4. Call the police, please. _____

5. Please wait for me. _____

6. Help me with my homework, please. _____

3 | AFFIRMATIVE AND NEGATIVE STATEMENTS WITH CAN

Read the information in the chart. Complete the sentences below. Use **can** *or* **can't** *and the words in parentheses.*

CAN THEY . . . ?	AMANDA	JUDY	STEVE	JOSH
Sing	yes	no	no	yes
Dance	yes	yes	no	no
Swim	yes	yes	yes	no
Play tennis	no	yes	no	no
Water ski	no	yes	no	no
Ice skate	no	no	yes	yes
Play the guitar	yes	no	no	yes
Play the piano	no	no	yes	yes

1. Amanda _____ _can sing_ _____, and she _____ _can dance_ _____.
   (sing)   (dance)

2. Josh _____ _can sing_ _____, but he _____ _can't dance_ _____.
   (sing)   (dance)

3. Steve and Josh _____, but they _____.
                  (water ski)   (ice skate)

4. Judy _____, and she _____.
        (play the guitar)   (play the piano)

5. Judy _____, and she _____.
        (swim)   (play tennis)

6. Steve and Amanda _____, but they _____.
        (swim)   (play tennis)

7. Amanda _____, and she _____.
        (water ski)   (ice skate)

8. Amanda _____, but she _____.
        (play the guitar)   (play the piano)

Now complete sentences about yourself.

9. I _____, _____ I _____.
        (sing)   (dance)

10. I _____, _____ I _____.
        (swim)   (play tennis)

4 | YES / NO QUESTIONS WITH *CAN*

*Write questions with **can**. Then write short answers. Use the information in parentheses.*

1. **A:** *Can Blanca speak Spanish well?* _____

   B: *Yes, she can.* _____ (Blanca can speak Spanish well.)

2. **A:** _____

   B: _____ (I can't speak French.)

3. **A:** _____

   B: _____ (Mike can't play the piano.)

4. **A:** _____

   B: _____ (Rosie can't understand Italian.)

5. **A:** _____

   B: _____ (The doctor can see you tomorrow.)

6. **A:** _____

   B: _____ (I can't go shopping with you today.)

5 | WH- QUESTIONS WITH CAN

Write questions. Use the words in parentheses and **can**. *Then write true short answers.*

1. (Where / I / get a good pizza)

   <u>Where can I get a good pizza?</u>   <u>At Gino's Pizzeria.</u>

2. (How / I / learn your language)

   _____   _____

3. (Who / cut my hair)

   _____   _____

4. (Where / I / buy CDs)

   _____   _____

5. (What / I / do on the weekend in your town)

   _____   _____

6 | EDITING

Correct the conversation. There are eight mistakes. The first mistake is already corrected.

                   Can you

A: I have a problem. ~~You can~~ help me?

B: Sure. How do can I help?

A: I can't not understand the homework. Can you understand it?

B: Yes, I do. But I can't to explain it well. Cans the teacher explain it to you?

A: I can't to find him.

B: He's in his office. I'm sure he can helps you.

The Simple Past: Regular Verbs (Statements)

1 | AFFIRMATIVE AND NEGATIVE STATEMENTS WITH THE SIMPLE PAST

*Read the sentences. Write **T** for True or **F** for False.*

_____ **1.** I stayed home last night.

_____ **2.** I didn't miss class two weeks ago.

_____ **3.** The teacher arrived late to class last week.

_____ **4.** I started my homework a few minutes ago.

_____ **5.** I learned a lot in English class last week.

_____ **6.** It didn't rain yesterday.

_____ **7.** I didn't talk to my friends yesterday evening.

_____ **8.** I didn't want to get out of bed yesterday morning.

2 | AFFIRMATIVE STATEMENTS WITH THE SIMPLE PAST

Complete the sentences. Use the simple past of the verbs in the box. Put a check (✓) next to the things you did last night.

bake listen play ~~talk~~ visit watch

_____ **1.** I _____*talked*_____ on the phone for a long time.

_____ **2.** I _____ TV all night.

_____ **3.** I _____ to the radio.

_____ **4.** I _____ bread.

_____ **5.** I _____ my grandparents.

_____ **6.** I _____ computer games.

3 | AFFIRMATIVE AND NEGATIVE STATEMENTS WITH THE SIMPLE PAST

Complete the sentences. Use the simple past.

1. I cook dinner at 6:00 every evening.

   I _____*cooked*_____ dinner at 6:00 yesterday evening.

2. I don't clean on Mondays.

   I _____*didn't clean*_____ last Monday.

3. Anton arrives on time every day.

   Anton _____ on time yesterday.

4. Tim doesn't cook.

   He _____ last night.

5. Steve enjoys his class.

   He _____ his class last week.

6. Yuko and Omar study at the library every morning.

   They _____ at the library yesterday morning.

7. We call our children every weekend.

   We _____ our children last weekend.

8. The students ask a lot of questions in every class.

   They _____ a lot of questions in class today.

9. We don't want to go to the movies late at night.

   We _____ to go to the movies late last night.

10. I don't buy shoes from that store.

    I _____ these shoes from that store.

4 | PAST TIME EXPRESSIONS

Complete the sentences. Use **yesterday**, **ago**, *or* **last**.

1. I watched a good movie _____*last*_____ night.

2. Maya missed class two days _____.

3. Juan wasn't late for class _____ morning.

4. Diego arrived in the United States _____ summer.

5. Claire left for Spain one week _____.

6. The party we went to _____ was fun.

7. The university was closed _____ Friday because of the weather.

8. We visited my grandparents _____ evening.

9. The weather wasn't so cold a month _____.

10. My friends and I studied until late _____ night.

5 | NEGATIVE STATEMENTS WITH THE SIMPLE PAST

Complete the sentences. Use the negative simple past of the verb.

1. I visited my parents, but I _____*didn't visit*_____ my grandparents.

2. I watched TV, but I _____ a DVD.

3. She talked to her brother, but she _____ to her sister.

4. They enjoyed the movie, but they _____ the book.

5. We played golf, but we _____ chess.

6. He learned French, but he _____ Spanish.

6 | PRONUNCIATION OF REGULAR PAST TENSE ENDINGS

Read the sentences. Check (✓) the sound of the past tense ending in the underlined word.

		/t/	/d/	/ɪd/
1.	Samantha <u>finished</u> school last year.	✓		
2.	Javier <u>arrived</u> in New York three months ago.			
3.	The class <u>ended</u> early.			
4.	Mark <u>stopped</u> to get some milk.			
5.	Lisa <u>wanted</u> to go to Mexico.			
6.	We <u>looked</u> at the board.			
7.	The Smiths <u>enjoyed</u> the party.			
8.	Sherry <u>talked</u> to Ben on the phone.			
9.	I <u>stayed</u> home last night.			
10.	Daniel <u>studied</u> all weekend.			
11.	Lars <u>visited</u> his friend last Saturday.			
12.	Paul <u>missed</u> the bus this morning.			
13.	Sonia <u>needed</u> a ride to work yesterday.			
14.	Joe <u>smiled</u> at me.			
15.	We <u>waited</u> for the show to start.			

7 | EDITING

Correct the e-mail message. There are six mistakes. The first mistake is already corrected.

Subj: Rita Jonas
Date: September 7   9:52 P.M.
From: h.Okun@adsu.com
To: t.Olson@adsu.com

_____

          enjoyed
Thanks for dinner last week. I ~~enjoy~~ it very much. I hope I not talk too much. I

was liked your kids a lot. Jeremy did show me some great computer games.

    I talked to Rita's secretary again yesterday, but Rita didn't returned my call.

—Herb

P.S. Sorry I didn't thanked you before, but I was very busy.

The Simple Past: Regular and Irregular Verbs; Yes / No Questions

1 | REGULAR VS. IRREGULAR VERBS WITH THE SIMPLE PAST

Complete the chart. Write the base form of the verb. Check (✓) **Regular verb** *or* **Irregular verb**.

		BASE FORM OF VERB	REGULAR VERB	IRREGULAR VERB
1.	I <u>went</u> to a party last night.	*go*		✓
2.	I <u>arrived</u> late.	*arrive*	✓	
3.	Sam and Tanya <u>came</u> late too.			
4.	They <u>left</u> early.			
5.	I also <u>saw</u> Miranda at the party.			
6.	She <u>played</u> the guitar with Tom.			
7.	I <u>enjoyed</u> the music.			
8.	The food <u>was</u> great too.			
9.	I <u>ate</u> a lot.			
10.	I really <u>liked</u> the pizza.			
11.	I <u>talked</u> to a lot of old friends.			
12.	I <u>had</u> a lot of fun.			
13.	The party <u>ended</u> after midnight.			
14.	I <u>got</u> home at around 1:30 A.M.			

2 | AFFIRMATIVE AND NEGATIVE STATEMENTS WITH IRREGULAR VERBS

Complete the sentences about yourself. Use the affirmative or negative simple past forms of the verbs in parentheses.

1. I _____*got up*_____ early yesterday.
   (get up)

2. I _____ a test last week.
   (take)

3. I _____ well last night.
   (sleep)

4. My teacher _____ to my home last weekend.
   (come)

5. A friend _____ me a gift two days ago.
   (buy)

6. My family _____ on vacation last month.
   (go)

3 | AFFIRMATIVE STATEMENTS WITH IRREGULAR VERBS

Change the sentences to the simple past. Write about the day in parentheses.

1. I have breakfast every morning.

   (today) *I had breakfast this morning.* OR *I had breakfast today.* _____

2. Sarah eats lunch every day.

   (today) _____

3. Matthew reads the paper every morning.

   (today) _____

4. Yoshi sleeps eight hours every night.

   (yesterday) _____

5. Jay and Diego go to the library every day.

   (yesterday) _____

6. I go to work every Saturday.

   (last Saturday) _____

4 | NEGATIVE STATEMENTS WITH IRREGULAR VERBS

Change the sentences to the simple past.

1. Makiko doesn't do her homework. *Makiko didn't do her homework.*

2. Henry doesn't go to bed at 8:00. _____

3. Maria doesn't buy breakfast at school. _____

4. John and Mary don't read the paper. _____

5. Linda doesn't get up at 6:00. _____

5 | YES / NO QUESTIONS AND SHORT ANSWERS WITH THE SIMPLE PAST

Write yes / no *questions. Then write short answers. Use the information in parentheses.*

1. **A:** *Did you wake up late yesterday?* _____

   B: *Yes, I did.* _____ (You woke up late yesterday.)

2. **A:** _____

   B: _____ (The teacher drank coffee in class last week.)

3. **A:** _____

   B: _____ (My friends and I didn't go out last week.)

4. **A:** _____

   B: _____ (Robert didn't eat breakfast today.)

5. **A:** _____

   B: _____ (Zai and Jeffrey took the bus today.)

6. **A:** _____

   B: _____ (My friends didn't come to my home last week.)

7. **A:** _____

   B: _____ (My friends bought ice cream today.)

6 | EDITING

Correct the conversations. There are seven mistakes. The first mistake is already corrected.

1. **A:** ~~You did~~ *Did you* sleep well last night?

   B: No, I wasn't.

2. **A:** I go on a picnic last Saturday.

   B: Did you have fun?

3. **A:** Did you eat anything at the party last night?

   B: No, and I not drink anything either.

4. **A:** I didn't saw my keys on the table.

   B: We putted them in your bag.

5. **A:** Did you went to school yesterday?

   B: Yes, I went to school.

7 | CONVERSATION COMPLETION

Complete the conversation. Use the words in the box. Don't look at your Student Book.

ate	didn't	snow	~~were~~
called	drank	Was	you
Did	happened	went	you're

KATHY: Hi, Amanda. Say, where ___*were*___ you and
                                    1.
Josh on the weekend? I _____ and left a
                        2.
message.

AMANDA: Well, we had an adventure!

KATHY: You did?

AMANDA: Yes. We _____ out of town on Saturday.
                    3.
We left at 3:00. About 4:00 it started to

_____ . In half an hour the snow was really
   4.
deep.

KATHY: Oh no! Did _____ stop?
5.

AMANDA: Yeah. We had to. I tried to call for help, but my cell

phone was dead. Then it got dark. We put on all our

warm clothes, so we were OK.

KATHY: _____ you have anything to eat?
6.

AMANDA: Yes, we did, actually. We had some cookies and

chocolate bars. We _____ those right away.
7.

And we had some water. We _____ it
8.

during the night.

KATHY: _____ it cold?
9.

AMANDA: Freezing! Fortunately, we had our sleeping bags. But

we _____ sleep much.
10.

KATHY: Then what _____?
11.

AMANDA: In the morning a snowplow came along and cleared

the road.

KATHY: Wow! That's scary. I'm glad _____ OK.
12.

AMANDA: Thanks. Me too.

1 | *WH-* QUESTIONS WITH THE SIMPLE PAST

Match the questions and answers.

__d__ 1. What time did you get up?

_____ 2. What did you have for breakfast?

_____ 3. Who made you breakfast?

_____ 4. What did you do after breakfast?

_____ 5. How did you get to the beach?

_____ 6. Where did you have lunch?

a. A bagel and fruit.

b. At the beach.

c. We took the bus.

~~**d.**~~ At 7:30.

e. My mother.

f. We went to the beach.

2 | AFFIRMATIVE AND NEGATIVE STATEMENTS WITH THE SIMPLE PAST

Complete the paragraph. Use the simple past of the verbs in parentheses.

The accident at First and Main _____*happened*_____ at 8:02. The driver of a black BMW
                                     1. (happen)

_____ at a red light. The driver of a white Toyota _____
     2. (not / stop)   **3. (not / see)**

the BMW. The driver of the Toyota _____ the BMW. The drivers
                                             4. (hit)

_____ out of their cars. They _____ a fight. Two men on
     5. (get)   **6. (have)**

the street _____ the fight. A woman _____ the accident

7. (stop)   8. (see)

and _____ the police. They _____ to the accident quickly.

9. (call)   10. (come)

3 | WH- QUESTIONS WITH THE SIMPLE PAST

Complete the conversation. Write questions about the accident in Exercise 2. Use **what**, **when**, **where**, **who**, *or* **why** *and the verbs in parentheses. Use the information in the answers to help you.*

1. **A:** (happen) _Where did the accident happen?_ _____

   B: At First and Main.

2. **A:** (happen) _____

   B: At 8:02.

3. **A:** (not / stop) _____

   B: The driver of a black BMW.

4. **A:** (hit) _____

   B: The driver of a white Toyota.

5. **A:** (get out) _____

   B: Both drivers got out of their cars.

6. **A:** (have) _____

   B: A fight.

7. **A:** (stop) _____

   B: Two men on the street.

8. **A:** (call) _____

   B: A woman did.

4 | STATEMENTS AND QUESTIONS WITH THE SIMPLE PAST

Complete the conversation. Use the simple past of the words in parentheses. Use **did** *in questions where necessary.*

AMANDA: _____*I called*_____ you on the weekend, but _____ home.
　　　　　　　　1. (I / call)　　　　　　　　　　　　　　　　　　2. (you / not be)

　　　　　Where _____?
　　　　　　　　　3. (you / go)

KATHY: _____ to Mark's parents' house.
　　　　　4. (we / go)

AMANDA: Oh? _____ there all weekend?
　　　　　　　　5. (you / stay)

KATHY: Yes. _____ two nights there. _____ there on
　　　　　　　6. (we / spend)　　　　　　　　　　　　7. (we / fly)

　　　Friday night and back last night.

AMANDA: What _____ there?
　　　　　　　　8. (you / do)

KATHY: Well, on Saturday morning _____ home with Mark's parents and
　　　　　　　　　　　　　　　9. (we / stay)

　　　_____.
　　　10. (talk)

AMANDA: What _____ about?
　　　　　　　　11. (you / talk)

KATHY: Lots of different things. _____ about funny things
　　　　　　　　　　　　　　12. (I / learn)

　　　_____ as a child and about other people in his family.
　　　13. (Mark / do)

AMANDA: _____ anybody else in the family?
　　　　　14. (you / meet)

KATHY: Yeah. In the evening, _____ a party for us.
　　　　　　　　　　　　　15. (they / have)

AMANDA: Who _____?
　　　　　　　16. (come)

KATHY: A lot of people—aunts, uncles, and cousins.

AMANDA: So _____ the whole family?
　　　　　　　17. (you / meet)

KATHY: Just about.

AMANDA: _____ fun?
　　　　　18. (it / be)

KATHY: Oh, yeah. _____ myself a lot.
　　　　　　　　　19. (I / enjoy)

5 | EDITING

Correct the conversations. There are nine mistakes. The first mistake is already corrected.

1. **A:** What ~~had we~~ ^{*did we have*} for homework?

   B: Pages 90 and 91.

2. **A:** Who did build your house?

   B: My grandfather builded it.

3. **A:** Why did you got a letter from Steven Spielberg?

   B: Because I writed him and he answered my letter.

4. **A:** What happened at the game?

   B: The other team win.

5. **A:** What time the game began?

   B: It began late, at 2:30, because it rained.

6. **A:** How the party was?

   B: Oh, we had a great time.

6 | CONVERSATION COMPLETION

Complete the conversation. Use the words in the box. Don't look at your Student Book.

accident	dented	happened	What do you mean
auto repair shop	did	~~it's for you~~	What's worse
broke	happen	took	Why

JOSH: Amanda, _____*it's for you*_____. It's your brother.
   1.
He says it's important.

AMANDA: Thanks, Josh . . . Hi, Rob. What's up? . . . Oh no!

Are you OK? . . . When _____ it
   2.

happen? . . . Where did it _____?
   3.

. . . Are you there now? . . . Why did you *drive* there?

_____ did you go *there*? . . . Does
   4.

Dad know? Sorry. I think Dad needs to know.

(continued)

[Amanda hangs up.]

JOSH: What _____ 5. ?

AMANDA: Rob had a car _____ 6. this morning.

JOSH: How is he?

AMANDA: He's fine, but the car isn't. He wanted to get some videos, and he didn't want to walk to the store. He _____ 7. Dad's car. Anyway, he saw a parking spot in front of the video store. He tried to park there and accidentally hit a sign. He _____ 8. the headlights and _____ 9. the bumper.

JOSH: That's too bad.

AMANDA: _____ 10. , he drove Dad's car without Dad's OK.

JOSH: Uh-oh.

AMANDA: He didn't want to go to Dad's _____ 11. . He's at a new body shop. This body shop wants $600 to fix the car today.

JOSH: Poor Dad.

AMANDA: _____ 12. "poor Dad"? Poor Rob.

Subject and Object Pronouns

1 | SUBJECT AND OBJECT PRONOUNS

Write a conversation. Use the sentences in the box.

> How about a tennis racket?
>
> Hmm. What does she like?
>
> Then why don't you get her a gift card?
>
> Happy to help you.
>
> They are too expensive.
>
> ~~It's my friend's birthday tomorrow. What's a good gift for her?~~
>
> That's a good idea. I'll get her a gift card at a sporting goods store! Thanks!
>
> Well, she likes sports.

A: *It's my friend's birthday tomorrow. What's a good gift for her?*

B: _____

A: _____

B: _____

A: _____

B: _____

A: _____

B: _____

2 | SUBJECT PRONOUNS

Rewrite the sentences. Use subject pronouns.

1. Kathy gives Carlos and Tomiko a ride.   *She gives Carlos and Tomiko a ride.*

2. Carlos needs a gift idea. _____

3. My friends and I want to go to the party. _____

4. A CD is not an appropriate gift. _____

5. Bill likes nuts and chocolate. _____

6. Carlos's wife didn't go to the party. _____

3 | OBJECT PRONOUNS

Rewrite the sentences. Use object pronouns.

1. I didn't see Carlos.   *I didn't see him.*

2. Kathy drove the car to the party. _____

3. I talked to Bill and Carlos. _____

4. I didn't see Tomiko or Carlos's wife. _____

5. Bill loves chocolate. _____

6. Bill talked to me and my friend. _____

4 | OBJECT PRONOUNS

Complete the conversations. Use **me**, **you**, **him**, **her**, **it**, **us**, *or* **them**.

1. **A:** Here, Bill. This gift is for _____*you*_____.

   B: Thanks a lot.

2. **A:** Is this gift appropriate for Bill?

   B: Yes, I think it's OK to give _____ chocolates.

3. **A:** How did you get here? Did Kathy give _____ a ride?

   B: No. Carlos brought _____.

4. **A:** You walked all the way here? You're kidding! I don't believe _____.

   B: It's true. Walking is nice. I love _____.

5. **A:** Carlos, can I use your cell phone?

   B: I don't have _____ here.

6. **A:** Does Carlos know your wife?

   B: Yes. He's talking to _____ right now.

7. **A:** Tomiko, do you like these earrings?

   B: Yes, I like _____ very much.

8. **A:** You and your girlfriend didn't come to the party.

   B: That's because nobody invited _____.

5 | SUBJECT AND OBJECT PRONOUNS

Complete the conversations with subject and object pronouns.

1. **A:** Where are the chips?

   B: _____*They*_____ are in the dining room. I put _____*them*_____ on the table.

2. **A:** Did you invite Carlos and Tomiko? I like _____.

   B: Yes, _____ are coming with Kathy. _____ has a car.

3. **A:** Did you invite Mark?

   B: I invited _____, but _____ can't come.

4. **A:** This chair is heavy. I can't move _____. Can you help _____?

   B: Sure.

5. **A:** Oh, somebody's at the door. Can you open _____?

   B: _____'s already open.

6. **A:** Hello, Tomiko. It's nice to meet _____. Bill talks about _____ all the time.

   B: Really? Does _____ say nice things?

7. **A:** Bill, Tomiko is thirsty. Can you bring _____ a soda, please?

   B: But _____ is drinking some soda right now.

8. **A:** Bill, there are chocolates on the table. Are they for _____?

   B: Yes, Carlos bought _____ for you and me.

6 | EDITING

Correct the note. There are eight mistakes. The first mistake is already corrected.

Dear Anne,

    Thank you for inviting ~~we~~ ^{us} to the party. The children and me had a great time. The games were great. The kids loved they.

    Did Bob and Sally find the gifts? I left it in their room. Did Bob like the tennis racket? I bought it at Central Sports for he. I got Sally's soccer ball there too. Does her still play soccer? (I know you said "No gifts," but what's a birthday without gifts?)

    Why don't us meet one day for lunch? Give I a call.

Talk to you soon,

Sarah

7 | CONVERSATION COMPLETION

Complete the conversation. Use the words in the box. Don't look at your Student Book.

~~For~~	her	I	so	to	you
He	him	me	them	us	your

CARLOS: Kathy, you're an American. What's a good gift?

KATHY: _____For_____ what?
       1.

CARLOS: For the party at Bill's house on Saturday. I want to get _____ a gift.
                                                                    2.

KATHY: Right. Let me think.

CARLOS: How about flowers?

KATHY: Well, I suppose _____. But you don't usually give flowers _____
                        3.   **4.**

       a man.

CARLOS: _____ has a wife. Can I give them to _____?
         5.   **6.**

KATHY: Hmm. I'm not sure.

CARLOS: What about a CD of some cool Latin music? I know he likes music.

KATHY: No. Not appropriate. You don't give _____ boss a CD.
                                            7.

CARLOS: Well, what do you suggest?

KATHY: Why don't you give them some chocolates? He's always eating _____
                                                                     8.

       at his desk.

CARLOS: OK, good idea. A box of chocolates. Now, another question.

KATHY: What?

CARLOS: Tomiko and _____ need a ride to the party. Can you take _____?
                    9.   **10.**

KATHY: For a price.

CARLOS: For a price? What do you mean?

KATHY: Get _____ a box of chocolates too.
            11.

CARLOS: I don't believe you. You're not serious, are you?

KATHY: No, just kidding! I'll pick _____ up at 6:30 on Saturday.
                                    12.

25 How much / How many; Quantity Expressions

1 | HOW MUCH / HOW MANY

Answer the questions about your last vacation. Use a number or choose from the short answers in the box.

A lot.	None.	Not many.	Not much.

1. How many days were you away? _____

2. How much money did you spend? _____

3. How many postcards did you send? _____

4. How many photos did you take? _____

5. How many people were with you? _____

6. How many bags did you take? _____

7. How much swimming did you do? _____

8. How many different restaurants did you eat at? _____

9. How much time were you alone? _____

2 | HOW MUCH / HOW MANY

Write a conversation. Use the sentences in the box.

> Just a little, because the food wasn't great. But the prices were good.
>
> ~~How was the restaurant?~~
>
> How many people were there?
>
> Not much—only $30 for all of us.
>
> It was OK.
>
> How much did you eat?
>
> Four of us.
>
> Really? How much did you spend?

A: _How was the restaurant?_____

B: _____

A: _____

B: _____

A: _____

B: _____

A: _____

B: _____

3 | GENERAL QUANTITY EXPRESSIONS

Circle the letter of the best answer.

1. How many workers does the hotel have?

    (a.) Many.   **b.** Not much.   **c.** A little.

2. How many parking spaces does the hotel have?

    a. Much.   **b.** Not much.   **c.** Not many.

3. How many rooms does the hotel have?

    a. Much.   **b.** A lot.   **c.** A little.

4. How much money does it cost to stay at the hotel?

    a. A few.   **b.** Many.   **c.** Not much.

(continued)

5. How many days did you stay there?

   a. Much.　　　**b.** Not much.　　　**c.** A few.

6. How much furniture do the rooms have?

   a. Many.　　　**b.** Not much.　　　**c.** A few.

7. How many meals do people eat at the hotel?

   a. Not many.　　　**b.** Not much.　　　**c.** Much.

8. How much time do people spend in the swimming pool?

   a. A few.　　　**b.** Many.　　　**c.** A lot.

4 | *HOW MUCH / HOW MANY*

Look at the picture of Steve's refrigerator. Write questions. Use **how many** *or* **how much** *and the words in parentheses. Then write answers. Use* **a lot**, **not many**, *or* **not much**.

1. (potatoes)

<u>How many potatoes does Steve have?</u>   <u>A lot.</u>

2. (oranges)

_____   _____

3. (bananas)

_____   _____

4. (milk)

_____   _____

5. (apples)

_____   _____

6. (soda)

_____   _____

7. (yogurt)

_____   _____

8. (juice)

_____   _____

9. (eggs)

_____   _____

10. (food)

_____   _____

5 | EDITING

Correct the conversation. There are six mistakes. The first mistake is already corrected.

A: How ~~many~~ *much* time do you get for vacation?

B: Four weeks.

A: Do you spend lot of time at home during your vacation?

B: No, only a little days.

(continued)

A: Where do you usually go?

B: We spend a few time at my wife's parents' home. Then we go to the beach. We spend some time with our friends there.

A: How many friend do you see at the beach?

B: Not much. Four or five.

6 | CONVERSATION COMPLETION

Complete the conversation. Use the words in the box. Don't look at your Student Book.

a	did	~~How~~	much	people	was
bet	Don't ask	many	nothing	time	were

STEVE: Welcome back.

JESSICA: Thanks.

STEVE: _____*How*_____ was Ecuador?
　　　　　　　1.

JESSICA: Great.

STEVE: How _____ days were you away?
　　　　　　　　　　2.

JESSICA: Ten. We _____ in the capital,
　　　　　　　　　　　3.
Quito, and on the Galápagos Islands.

MARK: The Galápagos Islands? That sounds exciting. How much _____ did you
　　　　　　　　　　　　　　　　　　4.
spend there?

TIM: Not _____. Only four days. But it _____ fantastic. We took
　　　　　5.　　　　　　　　　　　　**6.**
about _____ hundred photos. And we ate and slept on a boat.
　　　　　7.

MARK: Really? How many _____ were on the boat?
　　　　　　　　　　　　8.

JESSICA: Twelve including us. All very interesting people.

STEVE: I'll _____. How much _____ the trip cost?
　　　　　9.　　　　　　　　**10.**

JESSICA: _____.
　　　　　11.

JUDY: Well, _____ beats travel.
　　　　　　12.

TIM: You said it.

There is / There are

1 | AFFIRMATIVE AND NEGATIVE STATEMENTS WITH *THERE IS / THERE ARE*

Look at the picture. Complete the sentences. Use **'s**, **isn't** *(or* **'s not**), **are**, *or* **aren't**.

1. There _'s_____ a window with a view.

2. There _'s not OR isn't_ a TV in the room.

3. There _____ cups on the table.

4. There _____ any glasses on the table.

5. There _____ a bathroom in the room.

6. There _____ a radio in the room.

7. There _____ any books in the room.

8. There _____ towels in the room.

9. There _____ a suitcase on the bed.

10. There _____ some pictures on the walls.

11. There _____ a desk in the room.

12. There _____ a mirror above the sink.

2 | AFFIRMATIVE AND NEGATIVE STATEMENTS WITH *THERE IS / THERE ARE*

Write sentences about your neighborhood. Use **there** *and the words in parentheses.*

1. (apartment building) _There are many apartment buildings in my neighborhood._

2. (supermarket) _There is a supermarket in my neighborhood._

3. (gym) _____

4. (post office) _____

5. (library) _____

6. (stores) _____

7. (park) _____

8. (bank) _____

9. (movie theaters) _____

10. (restaurants) _____

3 | QUESTIONS WITH *IS THERE / ARE THERE*

Put the words in the correct order. Write questions. Remember to add the correct capitalization.

1. station / nearby / an / is / there / Underground / ?

   Is there an Underground station nearby?

2. block / any / are / on / banks / there / this / ?

   _____

3. near / is / drugstore / a / here / there / ?

   _____

4. in / area / any / there / this / are / theaters / ?

   _____

5. many / area / museums / are / in / how / this / there / ?

   _____

6. can / are / take / there / buses / we / any / there / ?

   _____

7. theater / are / near / any / restaurants / there / the / good / ?

   _____

8. there / in / art / town / place / to / good / is / a / buy / ?

   _____

4 | QUESTIONS AND ANSWERS WITH *THERE IS / THERE ARE*

Complete the conversation. Use **there** *with* **is**, **are**, **isn't**, *or* **aren't**.

A: Soho is a good place to go.

B: _____*Are there*_____ interesting things to do there?
                    1.

A: Yes, _____.
              2.

B: _____ cheap places to stay?
              3.

A: No, _____ many. But it's fun to visit.
              4.

B: _____ a good restaurant to eat at?
              5.

A: Yes, _____.
              6.

B: _____ a tour we can take?
              7.

A: _____. Not today.
              8.

B: _____ an art museum we can visit?
              9.

A: _____. It's close to the Underground.
              10.

B: _____ a place where I can send an e-mail?
              11.

A: _____. You can go online at the library.
              12.

5 | EDITING

Correct the e-mail message. There are seven mistakes. The first mistake is already corrected.

Subj: Hello from Prague!
Date: Wednesday, June 3
From: akang@jahoo.com
  To: r.hudson@adsu.edu

Hi, Rob! Greetings from Prague! We are having a great time here. Our hotel is very

nice; ~~there's~~ *it's* a comfortable, reasonable place that is close to everything we want to see.

There's many things to see and do here. They is a fantastic museum not very far from

our room. We went to Old Town today. It's an unusual clock there. It is so interesting!

There are also a very old pub there. I think it's from the 1400s. Some people were

dancing there.

Let's see . . . are there anything else I want to tell you? Oh, yes! We crossed a very

beautiful, old, scary bridge yesterday. On the other side, it was a castle! It's so amazing

to be here. This place has a long, rich history.

I have to go now. We're going to see a movie tonight so we can relax. Say hi to

everyone for me.

Love,

Alison

---

6 | CONVERSATION COMPLETION

Complete the conversation. Use the words in the box. Don't look at your Student Book.

Are there	~~Lead the way~~	snack bar	there's
hold	pleasure	That's	They're
Is there	restaurants	There are	Underground

AMANDA: Well, Josh, here we are. Now what?

JOSH: We need to find a place to stay . . . There's an information booth over there. Let's

go ask.

AMANDA: OK, hon. _____Lead the way_____.
　　　　　　　　　　　　　1.

ATTENDANT: May I help you?

JOSH: Yes, thanks. We're looking for a place to stay. _____ any youth hostels
　　　　　　　　　　　　　　2.
around here?

ATTENDANT: Well, _____ one near here,
　　　　　　　　　　　　3.
but it's kind of late. _____
　　　　　　　　　　　　　　　　　　4.
probably full by now. What about a bed-and-breakfast?

JOSH: Aren't bed-and-breakfasts pretty expensive?

ATTENDANT: Not always. _____ a few
　　　　　　　　　　　　　　5.
inexpensive ones. Would you like me to check?

AMANDA: Please do.

ATTENDANT: Let me just call, then.

[*A few moments later*]

ATTENDANT: Good news. There's a nice bed-and-breakfast about half a kilometer from here, and they have a room. It's very reasonable. They can _____ it for an
　　　　　　　　　　　　　　　　　　　　　　　　　　　　　　6.
hour.

JOSH: _____ great! Can you tell us how to get there?
　　　　　　7.

ATTENDANT: There's an Underground station just outside. Take the Circle Line west three stops. Here's an _____ map.
　　　　　　　　　　　　　　8.

AMANDA: We're starved. Are there any good fast-food _____ around here?
　　　　　　　　　　　　　　　　　　　　　　　　　　9.

ATTENDANT: There's a nice _____ right there. _____
　　　　　　　　　　　　　10.　　　　　　　　　　　　　11.
anything else I can help you with?

AMANDA: No, but thank you very much.

ATTENDANT: My _____. Enjoy your stay in London.
　　　　　　　　12.

UNIT

27 Noun and Adjective Modifiers

1 | NOUN AND ADJECTIVE MODIFIERS

Circle the noun and adjective modifiers in the sentences.

1. Mr. Lee is a (fun-loving) man.

2. Sean is fun and romantic.

3. Cynthia likes spy movies.

4. Kevin is a computer science major.

5. Owen is an easygoing guy.

6. Pietro is an excellent soccer player.

7. Mrs. Kitagawa is artistic.

8. The class is lively and interesting.

9. Russell has a new winter jacket.

10. The Whites are going on an exciting vacation.

2 | SENTENCES WITH ADJECTIVE + NOUN

Complete the sentences. Use any adjectives that make sense.

1. I had _____Italian_____ food for dinner last night.

2. _____ cities are fun to visit.

3. _____ people make me angry.

4. I have a(n) _____ family.

5. Yesterday was a(n) _____ day.

6. I think _____ people are interesting.

7. China is a(n) _____ country.

8. I am a(n) _____ person.

3 | ADJECTIVE MODIFIERS

Combine the sentences.

1. He is an older man. He is fun-loving.

   He is a fun-loving older man.

2. Venus and Serena Williams are tennis players. They are famous.

   _____

3. Jessica and Tim live in a house. The house is big.

   _____

4. Josh and Amanda ate at a restaurant. The restaurant was awful.

   _____

5. Judy likes movies. The movies are sad.

   _____

6. Buy this CD player. The CD player is cool.

   _____

7. Jeremy bought a CD player. The CD player was expensive.

   _____

8. Bill and Mark have jobs. The jobs are important.

   _____

4 | ADJECTIVE MODIFIERS WITH PLURAL NOUNS

Rewrite the sentences. Make the nouns plural. Make all the other necessary changes.

1. The personal ad is funny. *The personal ads are funny.* _____

2. He is an interesting man. _____

3. The black dog is friendly. _____

4. The expensive car is over there. _____

5. The artistic student is a young Italian. _____

6. The boring book has a red cover. _____

7. The good-looking actor is from China. _____

5 | ADJECTIVE MODIFIERS

Write sentences. Use the words from columns A, D, and E only one time each.

A	B	C	D	E
~~Al Pacino~~			~~American~~	~~actor~~
Beijing and Mexico City			beautiful	artist
Ferraris and BMWs	is		big	book
Prince Harry and Prince William	are	(a)	British	cars
Quebec	was	(an)	expensive	cities
Sushi	were		Japanese	food
The Beatles			old	men
The Bible			poor	place
Van Gogh			young	singers

1. *Al Pacino is an American actor.*

2. _____

3. _____

4. _____

5. _____

6. _____

7. _____

8. _____

9. _____

6 | EDITING

Correct the conversation. There are seven mistakes. The first mistake is already corrected.

A: Where were you last night?

B: I had a date.

A: Really?

B: Yeah. I met ᵃ beautiful woman through a personal ad.

A: Oh, yeah? Tell me about her. Is she an athletic like you?

B: Yeah. She plays three differents sports.

A: What else?

B: Well, she's a person very funny, and she listens to olds songs like I do.

A: Does she work?

B: Yeah. She has a interesting job with a music company.

A: She sounds like she's the woman perfect for you.

B: She is.

1 | ADJECTIVES WITH ONE, TWO, OR MORE THAN TWO SYLLABLES

Write each word from the box in the correct column.

active	busy	difficult	friendly	honest	old
artistic	cold	exciting	funny	important	short
boring	dark	expensive	healthy	interesting	warm

ONE SYLLABLE	TWO SYLLABLES, ENDING IN -Y	TWO SYLLABLES, NOT ENDING IN -Y	MORE THAN TWO SYLLABLES
		active	

2 | REGULAR AND IRREGULAR COMPARATIVE ADJECTIVES

Write the comparative forms of the adjectives.

1. old _____older_____
2. funny _____
3. quick _____
4. bad _____
5. famous _____

6. good _____
7. important _____
8. expensive _____
9. heavy _____
10. hot _____

3 | COMPARATIVE ADJECTIVES

Complete the sentences. Use the comparative forms of the adjectives.

1. This book is interesting, but the other book is _____*more interesting*_____ .

2. I'm busy on Mondays, but I'm _____ on Tuesdays.

3. English is difficult, but Chinese is _____ .

4. Julia is short, but her sister is _____ .

5. The movie is funny, but the book is _____ .

6. The cake is good, but the ice cream is _____ .

7. This book is boring, but that book is _____ .

8. My grandfather is active, but my grandmother is _____ .

9. The traffic today is bad, but the traffic yesterday was _____ .

10. It's cold today, but it was _____ yesterday.

4 | COMPARATIVE ADJECTIVES + *THAN*

Make comparisons. Use the words in the box. Use each word only once.

bad	cheap	friendly	old	small
~~big~~	crowded	important	quick	warm

1. China is _____*bigger than*_____ Japan.

2. Good health is _____ money.

3. An airplane moves quickly. An airplane is _____ a car.

4. An adult is _____ a child.

5. The weather in Greece is _____ the weather in Canada.

6. A big city is _____ a small town.

7. A golf ball is _____ a soccer ball.

8. The traffic in big cities is _____ the traffic in small cities.

9. I can buy a bicycle, but I can't buy a car. A bicycle is _____ a car.

10. I like dogs more than cats. Dogs are _____ cats.

5 | QUESTIONS WITH *WHICH*

*Write questions about comparisons. Use **which** and the words in parentheses. Then write answers.*

1. (expensive / computers or cell phones)

   Which are more expensive, computers or cell phones?   *Computers.*

2. (easy / swimming or water skiing)

   _____   _____

3. (fast / planes or trains)

   _____   _____

4. (warm / India or Russia)

   _____   _____

5. (popular / around the world / soccer or baseball)

   _____   _____

6. (healthy / cake or fruit)

   _____   _____

6 | EDITING

Correct the conversation. There are eight mistakes. The first mistake is already corrected.

A: So how's your new apartment? Is it ~~more good~~ *better* than your old one?

B: Yes, it is. It's biger and more cheap.

A: And where is it? Is the location good?

B: Oh, yeah. It's near the train station, so it's more easy for me to get to work. And I like the

neighborhood too. It has a lot of trees and is beautifuler. It's also more cleaner.

A: How many bedrooms are there in your apartment?

B: Well, there are three bedrooms. One bedroom is smaller from the other two. It's noisyer too.

But the rest of the apartment is perfect. Why don't you come and see it this weekend?

A: That sounds like a good idea.

7 | CONVERSATION COMPLETION

Complete the conversation. Use the words in the box. Don't look at your Student Book.

~~about~~	cheaper	food	more	older	than
better	entertainment	got	of	real	worse

KEN: So when's the party?

LAURA: Saturday night at _____*about*_____ eight.
1.

MARTY: How many people are coming?

LAURA: I've _____ 15 on the list.
2.

MARTY: What about music? I can bring my rap and metal

CDs.

KEN: Get _____! We want to dance,
3.

right? Rap is bad for dancing, and metal is

_____.
4.

MI YOUNG: Let's have rock. It's a lot _____ for
5.

dancing.

LAURA: OK. My _____ brother has a lot of
6.

rock CDs. Now, what about _____?
7.

KEN: How about steak? We can barbecue some steak.

MI YOUNG: Let's get pizza. It's easier and quicker

_____ steak. And it's
8.

_____.
9.

KEN: OK, sounds good. And what about _____? Besides dancing, I mean.
10.

MARTY: How about watching some videos?

LAURA: Well . . . I'm tired _____ them. Games are _____
11.   12.

interesting than videos.

KEN: Hey, I know a really funny new game. It's called, "Who's faster? Who's smarter?

Who's funnier?" We can play that.

MI YOUNG: Sounds good.

UNIT 29 Superlative Adjectives

1 | REGULAR AND IRREGULAR COMPARATIVE AND SUPERLATIVE ADJECTIVES

Complete the chart.

	ADJECTIVE	COMPARATIVE	SUPERLATIVE
1.	*large*	*larger*	largest
2.	fast		
3.		more difficult	
4.			scariest
5.	hot		
6.		richer	
7.			friendliest
8.	important		
9.		kinder	
10.			worst
11.	easy		
12.		stranger	
13.			funniest
14.	good		
15.		smarter	
16.			warmest
17.	interesting		
18.		more dangerous	
19.			most delicious

2 | SUPERLATIVE ADJECTIVES

Compare the three things, places, or animals in the pictures. Use the words in parentheses.

Mercedes E500

MINI Cooper

Lincoln Navigator

1. (expensive / car) *The Mercedes E500 is the most expensive car.*

2. (small / car) _____

3. (large / car) _____

Quebec

Istanbul

New York

4. (cold / city) _____

5. (big / city) _____

6. (old / city) _____

Cheetahs

Elephants

Lions

7. (dangerous / animal) _____

8. (fast / animal) _____

9. (heavy / animal) _____

(continued)

Novel

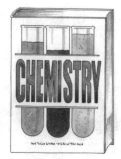

Textbook

Mystery

10. (exciting / book) _____

11. (romantic / book) _____

12. (boring / book) _____

3 | COMPARATIVE AND SUPERLATIVE ADJECTIVES

Complete the sentences. Use the comparative or superlative form of the adjective in parentheses.

1. The Nile is _____*the longest*_____ river in the world.
    (long)

2. The last unit was _____ this unit.
    (easy)

3. The Bluehouse Inn is _____ hotel by the lake.
    (good)

4. Prague was _____ city we visited.
    (interesting)

5. Asia is _____ continent in the world.
    (large)

6. The climate in Los Angeles is _____ the climate in New York.
    (warm)

7. Joe's Diner is _____ place to eat in my neighborhood.
    (bad)

8. The day we were in London was _____ of the year.
    (cold)

9. The final exam is _____ the test you took last week.
    (important)

10. _____ way to get to the airport is by taxi.
    (fast)

4 | EDITING

Correct the conversation. There are six mistakes. The first mistake is already corrected.

KATHY: Did you guys buy anything nice on the trip?

AMANDA: Well, Josh bought a new stamp for his collection. And I found these three blouses in an

open-air market. This pink one was ^*the* cheapest one I saw, and it was also prettier one.

KATHY: Yeah, it is pretty. Actually, I think that red one is the beautifulest.

AMANDA: Really? It was also the expensive one they had.

KATHY: Oh, wait! This white one is really beautiful too! Hmm, it's also the bigger one. It looks

too big for you.

AMANDA: You're right. I bought that one for you. I had to bring something home for best friend!

KATHY: Oh, Amanda! That's so kind of you. I love it. Thanks!

AMANDA: You're welcome.

5 | CONVERSATION COMPLETION

Complete the conversation. Use the words in the box. Don't look at your Student Book.

~~best~~	honking	most interesting	terrible
dangerous	hottest	rained	turned out
great	most exciting	scariest	worst

MARK: Welcome back, world travelers!

AMANDA: Thanks. We *feel* like world travelers.

KATHY: So come on—tell us all about it. What was the

_____*best*_____ thing about your trip?
1.

AMANDA: Well, for me it was just being in London. That was

the _____ place.
2.

JOSH: Yeah, London was _____. But
3.

Stonehenge was the _____ place we
4.

saw.

(continued)

AMANDA: Yes, but it was also the _____ part of
                                              5.
the trip. We camped out near Stonehenge. Did you

know this is the _____ summer in
                          6.
Europe in 10 years? There was no rain for weeks—

until the night we camped out. It _____
                                              7.
hard, and we got really wet. It was the most

_____ night I can remember.
         8.

MARK: You guys are always having adventures. Did

anything unusual happen on your trip?

AMANDA: The two _____ things happened when
                          9.
we were driving. Tell them, Josh.

JOSH: Well, we had a flat tire at night. But the most

_____ thing happened when I made a
         10.
turn on one of those traffic circles and ended up

going in the wrong direction. You know they drive

on the left there? Suddenly there were cars

everywhere—_____ their horns.
                    11.
I pulled off to the side of the road, and it

_____ OK.
         12.

MARK: Tell you what: If we ever take a trip together, let me

drive, all right?

Prepositions of Time:
In, On, At

1 | PREPOSITIONS OF TIME

*Write **at**, **in**, or **on** before each word or phrase.*

1. _on_ weeknights

2. ____ 2:15

3. ____ Thursdays

4. ____ October 24, 2004

5. ____ May

6. ____ the evening

7. ____ a few minutes

8. ____ June 1st

9. ____ 1990

10. ____ the morning

11. ____ lunchtime

12. ____ 4:00

13. ____ November 3rd

14. ____ about 3:00

15. ____ the 15th

2 | TIME EXPRESSIONS

*Answer the questions. Write true long answers. Use **at**, **in**, or **on**.*

1. What time do you get up? _I get up at 7:30 in the morning._

2. What time do you go to bed? _____

3. What year were you born? _____

4. What month were you born? _____

5. When is your birthday? _____

6. When did your parents get married? _____

7. What time does English class start and end? _____

8. What days do you have English class? _____

3 | PREPOSITIONS OF TIME

Complete the conversation. Use at, in, or on.

LIZA: I'd like information about flights to Vancouver.

AGENT: When would you like to go?

LIZA: I'm not sure. I'd like to go ___*in*___ September—either _____ September 19th or
           1.   2.
_____ September 20th.
   3.

AGENT: Well, September 19th is _____ a Sunday, so the ticket is cheaper. Tickets _____
                                        4.   5.
weekdays are more expensive than tickets _____ the weekends.
                                              6.

LIZA: Really? Well, when are there flights _____ Sunday, September 19th?
                                                    7.

AGENT: There's one _____ 7:00 _____ the morning, another _____ noon, one flight
                           8.   9.   10.
_____ the afternoon _____ 3:30, and another one _____ 9:00 _____
   11.   12.   13.   14.
night.

4 | DATES, TIME EXPRESSIONS, AND PREPOSITIONS OF TIME

Look at Josh's calendar. Complete the sentences on the next page.

NOVEMBER

Sunday	Monday	Tuesday	Wednesday	Thursday	Friday	Saturday
		1 library 7:00 P.M. gym	**2** 8:00 English class 2:00 math class	**3** museum with Diego	**4** library 7:00 P.M. gym	**5** soccer
6 soccer	**7** 8:00 English class	**8** library 7:00 P.M. gym	**9** 8:00 English class 2:00 math class 7:00 P.M. gym	**10** 7:00 P.M. gym	**11** library 7:00 P.M. gym	**12** soccer
13 soccer	**14** 8:00 English class 7:00 P.M. gym	**15** library	**16** 8:00 English class 2:00 math class	**17** Mom's birthday— She turns 45!	**18** library dentist appointment	**19** soccer
20 soccer	**21** 8:00 English class	**22** library	**23** 8:00 English class 2:00 math class	**24** 7:00 P.M. gym	**25** library soccer party	**26** soccer
27 soccer	**28** 8:00 English class	**29** library 7:00 P.M. gym	**30** 8:00 English class 2:00 math class			

1. Josh goes to math class ___*at*___ 2:00 _____*in the afternoon*_____ on Wednesdays.

2. Josh goes to the library _____.

3. Josh plays soccer _____.

4. Josh is going to the museum _____.

5. Josh has a soccer party _____.

6. Josh's mother's birthday is _____ Thursday, _____.

7. Josh's mother turns 45 _____ 2006.

8. Josh is studying English and Math _____ November.

9. Josh often goes to the gym _____.

10. Josh has a dentist appointment _____.

5 | EDITING

Correct the conversations. There are eight mistakes. The first mistake is already corrected.

1. **A:** When does class start?
   B: ~~On~~ *At* 2:00.

2. **A:** Is your birthday on May?

   B: Yes, it is. It's on May 20th.

3. **A:** Do you ever work at the night?

   B: Sometimes. But I usually work in morning.

4. **A:** When is your flight?

   B: It's in 5:00 at the morning.

5. **A:** What do you do in weekends?

   B: In Sundays I go to my grandparents' home for dinner.

6 | CONVERSATION COMPLETION

Complete the conversation. Use the words in the box. Don't look at your Student Book.

afternoon	back	fun	looking	Saturday	two-story
at	doing	in	on	~~This~~	yourselves

FELIX: Hello, Tim! _____*This*_____ is Felix Maxa. Do you

1.

remember me? We met _____ August on the train

2.

to Seattle.

TIM: Felix! Of course! It's great to hear from you. How are you

_____?

3.

FELIX: Wonderful. Say, I called to invite you and your wife to our house for a barbecue.

TIM: That sounds like _____. We'd really like that. When is it?

4.

FELIX: On _____, the 20th, in the _____.

5.   6.

TIM: I think we're free. But I need to check with Jessica. Can I call you _____?

7.

FELIX: Sure.

[Later—phone rings]

FELIX: Hello?

TIM: Hi, Felix. This is Tim. I e-mailed Jessica, and she e-mailed back. We're free

_____ the 20th. We can come to the barbecue.

8.

FELIX: Great!

TIM: What's the address?

FELIX: We're at 819 40th Avenue. From 45th, turn left on Stone Way and then right on 40th. It's

the third house on the right, a light blue _____.

9.

TIM: OK. What time?

FELIX: Come at about 2:30.

TIM: Great. Can we bring anything?

FELIX: Just _____.

10.

TIM: OK. Thanks a lot. I'm _____ forward to it. See you on Saturday

11.

_____ 2:30. Bye.

12.

The Future with *Be going to*: Statements

1 | PRESENT PROGRESSIVE VS. THE FUTURE WITH *BE GOING TO*

Look at the pictures. Circle the correct statements.

1. **a.** He's falling.
   b. He's going to fall.

2. **a.** It's raining.
   b. It's going to rain.

3. **a.** He's sleeping.
   b. He's going to sleep.

4. **a.** She's putting the book down.
   b. She's going to put the book down.

(continued)

143

5. **a.** He's watching TV.
   b. He's going to watch TV.

6. **a.** She's buying something.
   b. She's going to buy something.

2 | AFFIRMATIVE STATEMENTS WITH *BE GOING TO*

*Look at the pictures. What are the people going to do? Complete the sentences about the future. Use **going to** and the words in the box.*

buy some food	have a party	see a movie	~~swim~~
exercise	have lunch	sleep	teach

1. They're *going to swim.*

2. They're _____

3. He's _____

4. They're _____

5. He's _____

6. She's _____

7. He's _____

8. They're _____

3 | NEGATIVE STATEMENTS WITH *BE GOING TO*

Make negative sentences. Use **be going to** *and the verbs in parentheses.*

1. Mr. Olson <u>*isn't going to see* OR *'s not going to see*</u> the dentist this week. He saw the dentist last
   (see)
   week.

2. Jessica _____ too much money on a gift. She spent too much last
   (spend)
   time.

3. My friends and I _____ a movie tonight. We saw a movie last night.
   (watch)

4. Mr. James _____ class today. He's going to teach next week.
   (teach)

5. My parents and I _____ my grandparents this weekend. We're going
   (visit)
   to visit them next weekend.

6. Jeremy _____ a test next week. He's taking a test this week.
   (take)

4 | AFFIRMATIVE AND NEGATIVE STATEMENTS WITH *BE GOING TO*

*Write sentences about your activities next weekend. Use **be going to** and the words in parentheses.*

1. (clean my home) <u>I'm going to clean my home next weekend. OR I'm not going to clean my home next weekend.</u>

2. (eat out) _____

3. (go out with friends) _____

4. (go shopping) _____

5. (go to the movies) _____

6. (play soccer) _____

7. (study) _____

8. (visit relatives) _____

9. (wake up early) _____

10. (work) _____

5 | EDITING

Correct the paragraph. There are six mistakes. The first mistake is already corrected.

                                                    It's

I can't believe the course is almost over. ~~It~~ going to end in one week. Most of my classmates

are going return home, but some are no going to leave. Rana going to start a new job. Misha is

going to taking another course. Masao and Laura is going to get married, and I'm going to go to

their wedding.

6 | CONVERSATION COMPLETION

Complete the conversation. Use the words in the box. Don't look at your Student Book.

~~be~~ chill	come doing	faster going	have hurry	jam not	start to

LAURA: Ken, hurry up! We're going to ____be____ late!
                                       1.

KEN: What's the _____? It's just a silly little soccer game!
                            2.

LAURA: It's not silly, and it's not little. Sam's on the team! It's a big game. I think they're _____ to win.

3.

KEN: I know. That's what you told me. Is your brother a good player?

LAURA: He's really good.

KEN: Do I need an umbrella?

LAURA: No. It's _____ going to rain. . . . Come on.

4.

[*Later*]

LAURA: Can't you drive any _____?

5.

KEN: I'm already _____ the speed limit. But how

6.

_____ you like soccer so much?

7.

LAURA: It's a great game. A lot of people can play it. You don't

_____ to be a giant.

8.

KEN: But is it a real sport? Take basketball or baseball or football. Those are sports.

LAURA: Soccer is the most popular sport in the world.

KEN: Well, it's not the most popular sport in *my* world.

LAURA: Oh, no! A traffic _____! The game's going to

9.

_____ soon.

10.

KEN: Laura, _____ out! We're going _____

11.   12.

make it on time.

32 The Future with *Be going to*: Yes / No Questions

1 | YES / NO QUESTIONS WITH *BE GOING TO*

Match the questions and answers.

___e___ 1. Is Jeremy going to be late for school?   **a.** Yes, they're going to leave tomorrow.

_____ 2. Are you going to bed now?   **b.** Yes, you love Italian restaurants.

_____ 3. Are we going to go out to eat?   **c.** No, I'm taking the bus.

_____ 4. Are they going to take a trip?   **d.** Yes, she's going to play today.

_____ 5. Is the baby going to come with us?   ~~**e.**~~ No, he's going to be on time.

_____ 6. Is she going to drive you?   **f.** Yes, I'm tired.

_____ 7. Am I going to like the restaurant?   **g.** Yes, she is.

_____ 8. Is Annie going to play in the game?   **h.** No, Dad's cooking tonight.

2 | YES / NO QUESTIONS WITH *BE GOING TO*

Answer the questions. Write true short answers.

1. Are you going to go to bed before 10:00 tonight? _____ *Yes, I am.* OR *No, I'm not.* _____

2. Are you going to get up before 8:00 A.M. tomorrow? _____

3. Are you going to stay home all day tomorrow? _____

4. Are you going to watch TV this evening? _____

5. Are you going to eat dinner alone? _____

6. Are you going to go shopping this week? _____

7. Are you going to get some exercise today? _____

8. Are you going to do something interesting and unusual this month? _____

3 | FUTURE TIME EXPRESSIONS

Imagine that it is Sunday, May 1, 2015. Complete the conversations. Use the words in the box.

in five days	in two years	~~next week~~
in three months	next month	next year

1. **A:** Are you going to finish school _____ *next week* _____?

   B: Yes. I graduate on May 8th.

2. **A:** Are they going to get married in 2017?

   B: Yes. Their wedding is _____.

3. **A:** We're going to take a vacation _____.

   B: I'm going to go on vacation in August too.

4. **A:** Is Emily going to move _____?

   B: Yes, on June 8th.

5. **A:** I'm going to visit you on May 6th.

   B: Great! I'll see you _____.

6. **A:** He's going to graduate in 2016.

   B: Is he going to start college _____ too?

4 | *YES / NO* QUESTIONS WITH *BE GOING TO*; SHORT ANSWERS

Write yes / no questions with **be going to**. *Then write short answers. Use the information in parentheses.*

1. **A:** *Is it going to be cold tonight?* _____

   B: ___*Yes, it is.*_____ (It's going to be cold tonight.)

2. **A:** _____

   B: _____ (Mrs. Olson is going to take the job.)

3. **A:** _____

   B: _____ (You and your classmates aren't going to study tomorrow.)

(continued)

4. A: _____

    B: _____ (Josh's parents are going to move next year.)

5. A: _____

    B: _____ (Tim is going to get a haircut.)

6. A: _____

    B: _____ (You're not going to stay in bed today.)

5 | EDITING

Correct the conversation. There are nine mistakes. The first mistake is already corrected.

MARY: Hi, Annie. It's Grandma. How are you?

ANNIE: OK. Grandma, are you going to visit us this weekend?

MARY: No, I'm not going. I going to visit Uncle Steve.

ANNIE: Grandpa going to go with you?

MARY: Yes, he's. Why?

ANNIE: Because I'm bored. Mom is always at work, and we never do anything fun.

MARY: Let me talk to your mother.

ANNIE: She isn't here. She going being late tonight. Do you want to talk to Jeremy?

MARY: Why? Where's your dad? He is going to be late tonight too?

ANNIE: Yeah. They're both going to come home late.

MARY: Well, don't worry. I'm go to talk to both of them.

6 | CONVERSATION COMPLETION

Complete the conversation. Use the words in the box. Don't look at your Student Book.

Actually	be	~~How~~	Is	It's	Not bad
Are	going	I'm	isn't	matter of fact	was

JESSICA: _____*How*_____ was work, Tim?
1.

TIM: _____. How _____
2.   3.

your day?

JESSICA: _____, I had an interesting call.
4.

TIM: Oh?

JESSICA: You know Dan Evans, the TV producer?

TIM: Sure I do.

JESSICA: Well, he has an idea for a new show.

TIM: Really?

JESSICA: Uh-huh. _____ going to be on national TV, and he wants me to be in it.
5.

JEREMY: Awesome! _____ you going to have a big part?
6.

JESSICA: As a _____, yes. I'm going to _____ the main reporter.
7.   8.

JEREMY: That's so cool.

TIM: Hmm . . . _____ it going to mean a lot of travel?
9.

JESSICA: I think so.

ANNIE: Don't take it, Mom. I don't want you to travel.

BEN: Yeah. You always help me with my homework. Who's _____ to help me
10.

with my homework?

TIM: Hey, guys. _____ still going to be here.
11.

JESSICA: Anyway, kids, this is all very new. The show _____ going to air for a
12.

long time.

33 The Future with *Be going to:* *Wh-* Questions

1 | QUESTION WORDS

Read the answers. Write the correct question words. Use **how, what, when, where, who,**
or **why.**

1. _____What_____ ?   Write a parking ticket.

2. _____ ?   The owner of the car.

3. _____ ?   At 5:00.

4. _____ ?   The woman's wallet.

5. _____ ?   Angry.

6. _____ ?   The man in the black shirt.

7. _____ ?   Because they're going to see a movie.

8. _____ ?   On a ski vacation.

2 | *WH-* QUESTIONS WITH *BE GOING TO*

Look at the picture. Write questions. Use the words in parentheses and **be going to.** *Then
find an answer in Exercise 1 for each question.*

1. (What / the police officer / do)

   What is the police officer going to do?   *Write a parking ticket.*

2. (Who / get / a ticket)

   _____   _____

3. (Who / take / something from the old woman)

   _____   _____

4. (What / the man in the black shirt / take)

   _____   _____

5. (How / the old woman / feel)

   _____   _____

6. (Where / the owner of the car / go)

   _____   _____

7. (Why / the people / go into the movie theater)

   _____   _____

8. (When / the movie / start)

   _____   _____

3 | WH- QUESTIONS WITH *BE GOING TO*

Answer the questions. Write true answers.

1. What time are you going to go to bed tonight? _____

2. What time are you going to wake up tomorrow? _____

3. Where are you going to go tomorrow? _____

4. How are you going to get there? _____

5. Who are you going to spend time with next weekend? _____

6. How is your next class going to be? _____

7. When is your next test going to be? _____

4 | *WH-* QUESTIONS WITH *BE GOING TO*

Complete the conversations. Write questions with **be going to.** *Use* **how, what, when, where,** *or* **who** *and the words in parentheses.*

1. **A:** Kathy and Mark got engaged last week.

   B: (get married) _When are they going to get married?_____

   A: Next June, I think.

2. **A:** Kathy's parents are going to have an engagement party for her and Mark.

   B: (invite) _____

   A: A bunch of people—lots of relatives and friends.

3. **A:** I'm going to go to the supermarket.

   B: (buy) _____

   A: Some soda, some ice cream, and some other things for the party.

4. **A:** We're going to go to the city next weekend.

   B: (get there) _____

   A: One of my friends is going to drive us.

5. **A:** Melissa is going to go on vacation soon.

   B: (go) _____

   A: To Thailand.

6. **A:** The house is very messy.

   B: (clean it) _____

   A: This weekend.

5 | EDITING

Correct the conversation. There are eight mistakes. The first mistake is already corrected.

A: Did you hear the news? Amanda's pregnant.

B: Really? When ~~she is~~ going to have the baby?
             is she

A: At the end of January. She's going to stopping work in the middle of December.

B: Are we going have a party for her?

A: Yes. We going to have it in early December.

B: Wow, Amanda and her husband are to have a baby!

A: It going to be very exciting for them.

B: What is she and Josh going to name the baby?

A: I have no idea.

B: Where they going to live? Their apartment is very small.

A: I think they're going to move.

6 | CONVERSATION COMPLETION

Complete the conversations. Use the words in the box. Don't look at your Student Book.

are	have	say	~~what's~~
Congratulations	How	took	yeah
engaged	marry	What	You're

KATHY: Mark, _____ *what's* _____ bothering you? You seem
1.
nervous.

MARK: I *am* nervous. _____ am I going to say
2.
this?

KATHY: Say what?

MARK: Well, I have something important to

_____.
3.

KATHY: Let me guess. . . . _____ going to give up
4.
chocolate. Or . . . maybe you're going to clean your

closet.

MARK: No. This is about us . . . Will you _____
5.
me?

KATHY: Well . . . I only have one thing to say.

MARK: Oh, no. What?

KATHY: What _____ you so long to ask?
6.

(continued)

[Later]

MARK: Hello?

JOSH: Hey, Mark. This is Josh. _____ are you
      7.

going to do on Sunday evening?

MARK: No plans. Why?

JOSH: A bunch of us _____ going to watch the
      8.

big game. Do you want to come over?

MARK: Well, sure. By the way, Kathy and I _____
      9.

some big news.

JOSH: Oh _____? What?
      10.

MARK: We're _____.
      11.

JOSH: What? That's great, man! _____!
      12.

MARK: Thanks. Tell you about it on Sunday. So what time is the

party going to start?

Workbook Answer Key

In this answer key, where the full form is given, the contraction is also acceptable. Where the contracted form is given, the full form is also acceptable, unless the exercise is about contractions.

UNIT 1 (pages 1–5)

1

2. b   **4.** b   **6.** a
3. a   **5.** a

2

1. Look at
2. Listen to / Look at
3. Look at / Read
4. Answer / Ask / Listen to / Look at
5. Ask / Answer
6. Circle / Underline / Write

3

2. Five   **5.** six   **8.** nine
3. three   **6.** three **9.** Two
4. ten   **7.** One   **10.** four

4

2. a truck   **6.** empty
3. a gas station **7.** turn right
4. a bus stop   **8.** turn left
5. a restaurant

5

2. A: ~~You no~~ *Don't* go straight. Turn left.
   B: Got it.
3. A: Please don't ~~you~~ close the window. It's hot!
   B: Sure. No problem.
4. A: ~~Drives~~ *Drive* one block. Then turn right.
   B: OK. Thanks.

6

2. Don't worry   **7.** Got it
3. Indian   **8.** Avenue
4. drive   **9.** Don't park
5. turn   **10.** the truck
6. the gas station

UNIT 2 (pages 6–10)

1

3. son / brother
4. daughter / sister / wife / mother
5. husband / father
6. son / brother
7. daughter / sister
8. son / brother

2

Across   **Down**
7. CD   **1.** tickets
8. door   **3.** dictionary
9. pencil   **4.** VCR
10. tapes   **5.** notebook
11. photos   **6.** window
12. books   **9.** pens
13. keys

3

2. It   **7.** They
3. I   **8.** It
4. It   **9.** We
5. She   **10.** They
6. He

4

2. f   **4.** g   **6.** c   **8.** d
3. a   **5.** b   **7.** h

5

2. This is your pencil.
3. Is this your ticket?
4. These are your keys.
5. This is my house.
6. Is this your apartment?
7. Are these your friends?
8. These are your seats.

6

2. a   **4.** b   **6.** a
3. b   **5.** a

7

2. A: ~~These are~~ *Are these* your keys?
    B: Yes. Thank you.

3. A: This is my car.
    B: ~~She~~ *It* is big.

4. A: ~~This~~ *These* are *my* books.
    B: Oh. Sorry.

5. A: These are my ~~pet~~ *pets*.
    B: They're nice.

6. A: Is this your sister?
    B: Yes, her name is Mary. ~~He~~ *She* is a teacher.

UNIT 3 (pages 11–15)

1

2. ✓   **5.** ✓   **8.** ✓
3. ✓   **7.** ✓

2

3. isn't   **5.** is   **7.** is
4. isn't   **6.** is   **8.** is

3

2. is   **5.** are   **8.** is
3. is   **6.** are   **9.** am
4. is   **7.** are   **10.** is

4

2. It is beautiful there.
3. She is not sad.
4. We are not here on business.
5. You are friendly.
6. They are not from Seattle.

5

2. We're from Tokyo.   **4.** I'm not the teacher.
3. They're not here.   **5.** He's my cousin.
   OR They aren't here.   **6.** You're from here.

6

2. isn't / 's   **5.** isn't / 's
3. isn't / 's   **6.** 're not / 're
4. 'm not / 'm

7

2. A: ~~The~~ *Is the* food good?
    B: ~~Is~~ *It's* delicious.

3. A: This ⌃*is* my cousin.
    B: ~~Are~~ *Is* she a student?

4. A: ~~Be~~ *Are* you from Mexico?
    B: No, we're ~~are~~ from Peru.

5. A: ~~Your~~ *Are your* cousins Amy and Mary ~~are~~ here on vacation?
    B: No, ~~they~~ *they're* here on business.

8

2. is   **6.** capital   **10.** delicious
3. They're   **7.** from   **11.** It's
4. not   **8.** am   **12.** I
5. Australia   **9.** clean

UNIT 4 (pages 16–20)

1

2. h   **4.** b   **6.** g   **8.** f
3. d   **5.** a   **7.** e

2

1. That   **4.** This / these / These
2. those / Those   **5.** this / this
3. this / that

3

2. That car is from Italy.
3. That child is from Canada.
4. That boy is from Egypt.
5. That dish is from Austria.

4

2. Those people are from Mexico.
3. Those girls are from Japan.
4. Those glasses are from Austria.
5. Those computers are from the United States.

5

2. my
3. Their
4. my OR our
5. His
6. My OR Our
7. her
8. Her

6

2. b
3. a
4. a
5. b
6. a

7

2. A: Are those ~~you're~~ *your* children?
   B: No they're my brother's ~~child~~ *children*.
3. A: Are ~~that~~ *those/these* your glasses?
   B: No, they're my ~~sunglass~~ *sunglasses*.
4. A: Those ~~person~~ *people* are teachers.
   B: ~~His~~ *Their* names are Steve Beck and Annie Macintosh.
5. A: ~~That is~~ *Is that* your cousin?
   B: Yes, ~~she~~ *her* name is Jessica.

8

2. How about
3. her
4. those
5. binoculars
6. huge
7. That's
8. your
9. building
10. its
11. It's
12. a great idea

UNIT 5 (pages 21–25)

1

Conversation 1
A: Who's that woman?
B: That's Amy. She's my teacher.
A: Is she a good teacher?
B: Yes. And she's friendly too.
A: What's her last name?
B: Diaz.

Conversation 2
A: Is that your wife?
B: Yes. Her name's Ellen.
A: What does she do?
B: She's a writer.
A: What does she write?
B: Travel books.

2

2. b
3. a
4. b

3

2. Is she your sister?
3. Who is that woman?
4. Is your father an engineer?
5. What is their last name?
6. What does your friend do?

4

2. Yes, I am. OR No, I'm not.
3. Yes, I am. OR No, I'm not.
4. Yes, she/he is. OR No, she/he isn't. OR No, she's/he's not.
5. Yes, she/he is. OR No, she/he isn't. OR No, she's/he's not.
6. Yes, it is. OR No, it isn't. OR No, it's not.
7. Yes, they are. OR No, they aren't. OR No, they're not.
8. Yes, we are. OR No, we aren't. OR No, we're not.

5

2. Ben.
3. My grandchildren.
4. A key.

6

2. That's my brother. OR He's my brother.
3. It's Canberra.
4. It's Lynn Martin.

7

2. A: ~~You~~ *Are you* and Joe married?
   B: Yes, ~~we're~~ *we are*.
3. A: Who ~~be~~ *is* that boy?
   B: ~~That~~ *That's* my son.
4. A: ~~Who~~ *What* is the capital of the United States?
   B: ~~Is~~ *It's* Washington, D.C.
5. A: ~~That~~ *Is that* woman your mother?
   B: Yes, ~~she's~~ *she is*.
6. A: *Is* ^Bob a travel agent ~~is~~?
   B: No, he isn't.

8

2. you
3. Boy
4. it
5. Who's
6. Is
7. does
8. He's
9. Her
10. she
11. she's
12. What

UNIT 6 (pages 26–31)

1

2. hospital
3. restaurant
4. museum
5. library
6. movie theater

2

3. T
4. F
5. F
6. F
7. T
8. T

3

2. post office
3. restaurant
4. art museum
5. movie theater
6. park
7. supermarket
8. apartment building
9. library

4

2. Where are Mr. and Mrs. Lin from?
3. Where are the doctors from?
4. Where's Paul from? OR Where is Paul from?
5. Where are you from?

5

	Number	Word	Ordinal Number	Ordinal Word
1.	4	*four*	4th	*fourth*
2.	6	*six*	6th	*sixth*
3.	1	*one*	1st	first
4.	9	*nine*	9th	*ninth*
5.	8	*eight*	8th	*eighth*
6.	2	*two*	2nd	second
7.	3	*three*	3rd	*third*
8.	7	*seven*	7th	*seventh*
9.	10	*ten*	10th	tenth
10.	5	*five*	5th	*fifth*

6

2. It's on the first floor.
3. It's on the third floor.
4. It's on the fourth floor.
5. It's on the sixth floor.
6. It's on the second floor.

7

Hi Paula,

What's your phone number, and ~~what's~~ *where's* your apartment? Is it on Main Street? And what floor is your apartment ~~in~~ *on*?

Bob

Hi, Bob,

My phone number ^*is* 555-0900. My apartment isn't ~~at~~ *on* Main Street. It's ~~on~~ *at* 212 Park Avenue. Take the number 12 bus. My apartment building is next *to* ^the post office, and my apartment is on the ~~nine~~ *ninth* floor.

Paula

UNIT 7 (pages 32–36)

1

Answers will vary.

2

2. a   **4.** c
3. d   **5.** b

3

3. [I'm happy today, but] I wasn't happy yesterday.
4. [It's cold today, but] it wasn't cold yesterday.
5. [The children are not at a soccer game today, but] they were at a soccer game yesterday.
6. [We aren't tired today, but] we were tired yesterday.
7. [The streets aren't crowded today, but] they were crowded yesterday.
8. [You're at the library today, but] you weren't at the library yesterday.
9. [I'm not home today, but] I was home yesterday.
10. [The boys are at the movies today, but] they weren't at the movies yesterday.

4

2. wasn't   **5.** was   **8.** wasn't
3. was   **6.** was   **9.** were
4. were   **7.** weren't

5

2. A: Was Jeremy at a soccer game yesterday?
   B: Yes, he was.
3. A: Were Tim and Jessica at a play yesterday?
   B: Yes, they were.
4. A: Was Judy at a party last night?
   B: No, she wasn't.
   A: [Where] was she?
   B: At the movies. OR At a movie.
5. A: Was Mark at a soccer game yesterday?
   B: No, he wasn't.
   A: [Where] was he?
   B: At home.
6. A: Were Amy, Steve, and Jenny at a party last night?
   B: Yes, they were.

6

1. A: ~~They were~~ *Were they* at home yesterday?
   B: Yes, they ~~was~~ *were*.
2. A: Hi. ~~How~~ *How's* it going?
   B: Great.
3. A: ~~Were~~ *Was* the movie funny yesterday?
   B: No, it ~~isn't~~ *wasn't*.
4. A: Where were you ~~the~~ last night?
   B: ~~Was~~ *I was* at home.

7

2. How's   **6.** wasn't   **10.** great
3. last   **7.** movies   **11.** funny
4. weren't   **8.** alone   **12.** it
5. were   **9.** was

UNIT 8 (pages 37–41)

1

2. When   **6.** What
3. Where   **7.** How long
4. Who   **8.** Who
5. How

2

Answers to the following questions will vary.
2. How long was your English class?
3. When were you at the supermarket?
4. How was the weather yesterday?
5. Where were you yesterday?
6. Who were you with last weekend?

3

2. Fun. OR Great.
3. San Francisco. OR In San Francisco.
4. My brother and sister.
5. Five days. OR For five days.
6. Cool and rainy.

4

2. It was hot and rainy.
3. It was cold and sunny.
4. It was cold and cloudy.
5. It was warm and sunny.
6. It was cool and windy.

5

2. A: Who were the students *with*?
   B: They were with their teacher.

3. A: How long *was* class?
   B: Two hours.

4. A: How was the weather?
   B: ~~Was~~ *It was* sunny and warm.

5. A: When ~~was~~ *were* they here?
   B: Last Friday.

6. A: ~~Who~~ *What* movie was it?
   B: *Star Wars.*

6

2. you
3. long
4. wonderful
5. weather
6. cool
7. food
8. tour
9. was
10. Who
11. Remember
12. this

UNIT 9 (pages 42–46)

1

2. b
3. a
4. b
5. c
6. b
7. c
8. a

2

2. reports
3. teaches
4. likes
5. babysits
6. sings
7. play

3

2. doesn't have
3. don't speak
4. don't need
5. don't like
6. doesn't want
7. don't have
8. doesn't teach
9. doesn't rain

4

2. I drink coffee. OR I don't drink coffee.
3. I read newspapers. OR I don't read newspapers.
4. I go online. OR I don't go online.
5. I read novels. OR I don't read novels.
6. I study a lot. OR I don't study a lot.

5

2. look
3. don't look
4. have
5. has
6. work
7. works
8. work
9. doesn't work
10. goes
11. fixes
12. loves
13. doesn't love
14. speak
15. don't speak
16. speak
17. don't come
18. comes
19. comes
20. speaks
21. doesn't speak

6

My brother, Ken, ~~live~~ *lives* with my parents. They ~~lives~~ *live* in a big house. My father ~~have~~ *has* a new car. He cleans his car every day. Ken ~~not~~ *doesn't* have a new car. His car is old. It ~~don't~~ *doesn't* run, but he ~~love~~ *loves* it. My mother ~~no love~~ *doesn't love* cars. She ~~love~~ *loves* her garden. She ~~work~~ *works* in it every Saturday and Sunday. I ~~doesn't~~ *don't* see my family often, but we talk on the weekend.

7

2. go
3. lives
4. teaches
5. look
6. hair
7. eyes
8. likes
9. doesn't
10. watch
11. goes
12. sounds

UNIT 10 (pages 47–52)

1

3. J
4. B
5. B
6. J
7. B
8. B
9. J
10. B

2

2. f **4.** c **6.** e
3. b **5.** a

3

3. No, she doesn't.
4. No, they don't.
5. No, she doesn't.
6. Yes, they do.
7. Yes, she does.
8. Yes, I do. OR No, I don't.
9. Yes, I do. OR No, I don't.

4

2. Does she work on Sunday?
3. Does he speak Japanese?
4. Do they have a cat?
5. Does she know Kathy?
6. Do they need a new radio?
7. Does it have a library? OR Does the school have a library?
8. Do you speak Portuguese (at home)?

5

2. A: Does Mark need a haircut?
  B: Yes, he does.
3. A: Does Steve know a good hairstylist?
  B: Yes, he does.
4. A: Do you like coffee?
  B: No, I don't.
5. A: Does Mark speak Chinese?
  B: Yes, he does.
6. A: Does Nick go online and e-mail Mark?
  B: Yes, he does.
7. A: Does it rain a lot in September?
  B: No, it doesn't.
8. A: Does Judy want coffee?
  B: No, she doesn't.
9. A: Does Steve need an appointment?
  B: Yes, he does.

6

2. Does he read **6.** I love
3. Does your brother listen **7.** Jeremy doesn't like
4. That's **8.** Do you have
5. Do you like **9.** Jeremy loves

7

2. A: Does your grandmother ~~plays~~ *play* the guitar?
  B: Yes, she ~~is~~ *does*.
3. A: *Do your* ~~Your~~ three friends ~~do~~ play basketball?
  B: One friend ~~play~~ *plays* basketball. The other two play soccer.
4. A: *Does* ‸ *Focus on Grammar* have a lot of grammar practice?
  B: Yes, it ~~has~~ *does*.
5. A: Do you and the other students like this book?
  B: No, we don't ~~like~~.

8

2. Nothing much **8.** have
3. thinks **9.** Hold on
4. know **10.** haircut
5. charge **11.** think
6. reasonable **12.** like
7. need

UNIT 11 (pages 53–57)

1

2. g **5.** b **8.** c
3. f **6.** h
4. e **7.** a

2

2. goes to school
3. do you get to school?
4. do you talk about? *(Answers may vary.)*
5. does he go to school early?
6. does she get home?
7. do you play tennis?

3

2. It's seven-ten. OR It's ten after seven.
3. It's two (minutes) after three.
4. It's four-forty. OR It's twenty to five.
5. It's ten to nine. OR It's eight-fifty.
6. It's five to eight. OR It's seven fifty-five.
7. It's eleven o' clock. OR It's eleven.

8. It's one-thirty. OR It's half past one.
9. It's a quarter after two. OR It's two-fifteen.
10. It's a quarter to seven. OR It's six forty-five.
11. It's twenty-five after ten. OR It's ten twenty-five.
12. It's twenty-five to four. OR It's three thirty-five.

4

2. What does your mother do?
3. Why do you listen to jazz?
4. What time is dinner? OR What time do you eat dinner?
5. Why does he get up (so) early?
6. Where do your cousins live?
7. Who owns the restaurant?

5

YUKO: What time _{does} English class ~~starts~~ ^{start}?
OMAR: At 1:00.
YUKO: What time ^{does} class finish?
OMAR: At 2:30.
YUKO: What ~~means~~ *dislike* ^{does dislike mean}?
OMAR: It means "not like."
YUKO: How ^{do} you say this word?

OMAR: I don't know.
YUKO: ~~Do~~ ^{Does} the teacher teach every day?
OMAR: No. She doesn't teach on Friday.
YUKO: What ~~have we~~ ^{do we have} for homework?
OMAR: Page 97.
YUKO: Why does Elena know all the answers?
OMAR: She ~~study~~ ^{studies} a lot.

6

2. What	**6.** Why	**10.** off
3. work	**7.** time	**11.** does
4. late	**8.** sleep in	**12.** let's go
5. till	**9.** else	

UNIT 12 (pages 58–61)

1

2. isn't / has	**6.** isn't / has
3. aren't / don't have	**7.** isn't / has
4. is / doesn't have	**8.** is / doesn't have
5. are / have	

2

1. 'm OR 'm not
2. have OR don't have
3. 'm OR 'm not
4. have OR don't have
5. have OR don't have
6. 'm OR 'm not
7. have OR don't have
8. 'm OR 'm not
9. 'm OR 'm not
10. have OR don't have

3

2. is	**6.** is	**10.** have
3. is	**7.** has	**11.** have
4. isn't	**8.** doesn't have	**12.** are
5. is	**9.** is	

4

3. What's the name of Bono's band?
4. Is Bono a violinist?
5. What's Bono's real name?
6. Where is he from?
7. Does he have any brothers or sisters?
8. Is he married?
9. Do they have children?
10. Where do they have a home?

5

A: ~~What~~ ^{What's} your name?
B: Alice.

A: How old ~~have~~ ^{are} you?
B: I ~~have~~ ^{am} 24.

A: ~~You~~ ^{Do you} have a big family?
B: Yes, I do. I have three sisters and four brothers.

A: Where do you live?
B: My home ^{is} near here. It's on Center Street.

A: Is ^{it} big?
B: No. ~~It~~ ^{It's} small. I live alone. My family lives in another city.

A: ~~Have you~~ ^{Do you have} a job?
B: No. I study at a university.

6

2. these	6. She's	10. heads
3. look like	7. in	11. pregnant
4. has	8. doesn't	12. right away
5. are	9. unusual	

UNIT 13 (pages 62–66)

1

Answers will vary.

2

2. Steve does not exercise often.
3. Bill rarely eats at a restaurant.
4. It snows here sometimes. OR It sometimes snows here.
5. Mary is usually not busy. OR Mary is not busy, usually.
6. It is often hot in Cairo.

3

2. I sometimes play soccer. OR I play soccer sometimes.
3. I am rarely late for class.
4. The food at that restaurant is never good.
5. Jennifer rarely sees a play.
6. Robert often goes to the movies. OR Robert goes to the movies often.

4

2. Robert never cooks.
3. Nick usually goes to the gym. OR Usually, Nick goes to the gym. OR Nick goes to the gym, usually.
4. Mr. and Mrs. Lee sometimes go to a restaurant. OR Sometimes, Mr. and Mrs. Lee go to a restaurant. OR Mr. and Mrs. Lee go to a restaurant, sometimes.
5. Ruth always eats lunch.

5

2. Do you ever go to the theater?
3. Do your children ever stay home alone?
4. How often do you listen to the radio?
5. Do you ever smoke?
6. How often does Tim cook dinner?
7. Are you ever home on the weekend?

6

Hi, Sam,

Here is my schedule. I ~~usually am~~ *am usually* busy on Monday evenings. I ~~go often~~ *often go* to the gym, or I play basketball. (Do ~~ever you~~ *you ever* play basketball?) On Fridays ~~always I~~ *I always* exercise too. I go dancing at the club! On Wednesdays and Thursdays I sometimes work late, but I'm often free on Tuesdays. I finish *usually* work ~~usually~~ at 5:30. Do you want to meet at Vincenzo's Italian Restaurant at 6:30 on Tuesday? The food there is ~~good always~~ *always good*.

Bob

7

2. kind of	8. breakfast
3. sleep	9. hurry
4. about	10. always
5. usually	11. often
6. ever	12. times
7. Sometimes	

UNIT 14 (pages 67–70)

1

2. d	5. h	8. b
3. f	6. c	
4. g	7. a	

2

2. closing	6. fixing	10. opening
3. doing	7. looking	11. running
4. stopping	8. listening	12. trying
5. enjoying	9. moving	

3

2. are listening	6. is helping
3. reading	7. is working
4. is cooking	8. is answering
5. is washing	

4

2. I'm wearing glasses right now. OR I'm not wearing glasses right now.

3. I'm listening to music right now. OR I'm not listening to music right now.

4. I'm sitting in my bedroom right now. OR I'm not sitting in my bedroom right now.

5. I'm eating right now. OR I'm not eating right now.

6. I'm sitting with my friend right now. OR I'm not sitting with my friend right now.

7. I'm drinking water right now. OR I'm not drinking water right now.

8. I'm looking at a computer right now. OR I'm not looking at a computer right now.

5

Hello from Seattle. ~~It~~ *It's* raining right now, but ~~we have~~ *we're having* fun. Jenny and I are ~~sit~~ *sitting* in a restaurant. ~~I~~ *I'm* eating lunch. The food here in Seattle is good. Jenny ~~no is~~ *is not* eating. She ~~drink~~ *is drinking* coffee. We aren't ~~talk~~ *talking*. Jenny's ~~read~~ *reading* the newspaper. I hope you're fine.

6

2. studying
3. isn't studying
4. looking
5. 'm
6. watching
7. waiting
8. computer
9. Come on over
10. lasagna
11. is
12. See you soon

UNIT 15 (pages 71–74)

1

2. Yes, it is. OR No, it's not. OR No, it isn't.
3. Yes, it is. OR No, it's not. OR No, it isn't.
4. Yes, I am. OR No, I'm not.
5. Yes, they are. OR No, they aren't. OR No, they're not.
6. Yes, I am. OR No, I'm not.
7. Yes, I am. OR No, I'm not.
8. Yes, I am. OR No, I'm not.

2

2. A: Is he sleeping in his bedroom?
B: No, he isn't. OR No, he's not.
3. A: Are the Smiths eating dinner?
B: Yes, they are.
4. A: Is Ben doing his homework?
B: No, he isn't. OR No, he's not.
5. A: Are the children cleaning the kitchen?
B: No, they aren't. OR No, they're not.
6. A: Is Paula drinking coffee with milk?
B: Yes, she is.

3

3. Is Jessica cooking dinner? — Yes, she is.
4. Is the cat wearing a hat? — Yes, it is.
5. Are Ben and Annie playing cards? — Yes, they are.
6. Is Jeremy listening to music? — No, he isn't. OR No, he's not.
7. Is Tim writing a letter? — Yes, he is.
8. Is the cat sitting on the floor? — No, it isn't. OR No, it's not.
9. Is the cat reading? — Yes, it is.

4

2. He's making
3. Are your parents eating
4. My parents are having
5. Is he sleeping?
6. He's watching

5

1. A: Are you ~~sleep?~~ *sleeping*
B: No, ~~I~~ *I'm* not.
2. A: ~~The~~ *Is the* teacher giving us homework?
B: Yes, ~~she's.~~ *she is*
3. A: Is Mr. Olson ~~work?~~ *working*
B: No, he isn't. He's ~~eat~~ *eating* lunch.
4. A: Is ~~sleeping Kelly?~~ *Kelly sleeping*
B: No, she's not. ~~She~~ *She's* watching a DVD with her friend.

5. A: ~~Is~~ *Are* Tim and his boss wearing suits?

   B: Yes, ~~they're~~ *they are*.

6

2. watching	8. baking
3. babysitting	9. studying
4. everything	10. check
5. listening	11. cool
6. Everything's	12. be back
7. helping	

UNIT 16 (pages 75–78)

1

2. Who	5. Why	8. Where
3. What	6. How	9. Who
4. Where	7. What	10. What

2

2. Why are Jessica and Tim eating? — Because they're hungry.

3. What are the ducks doing? — They're swimming.

4. Where are Mary and Bill sitting? — On a bench.

5. How is everyone feeling? — Happy.

6. Where is Jeremy sitting? — On the grass by the pond.

7. Who is listening to music? — Jeremy.

8. What are Annie and Ben doing? — They're riding bikes.

3

2. Who are you talking [to]?
3. What are they baking?
4. Who is watching [the kids]?
5. Where is he studying?

4

2. A: What ^*are* the people watching?

   B: The soccer game.

3. A: Why ~~Mark is~~ *is Mark* wearing a suit?

   B: Because ~~he~~ *he's* going to a wedding.

4. A: ~~What's~~ *How's* everything going?

   B: Great. We are ~~have~~ *having* a lot of fun.

5. A: Where ^*are* Ben and Annie ~~are~~ going?

   B: To their grandmother's house.

6. A: Who's Jeremy ~~send~~ *sending* an e-mail message to?

   B: A friend from school.

5

2. Where's	6. Fish stew	10. What
3. Why	7. on	11. starved
4. out	8. I'm	12. why don't
5. What's	9. Who	

UNIT 17 (pages 79–82)

1

2. What are those? / Those

3. *Answers will vary. Possible answers include:*
   What does this / that say? OR What's this / that?

4. What's that? / That's

2

2. Diego's	4. Pam's
3. Gabrielle's	5. Josh's

3

2. His parents' names are Jessica and Tim.
3. Steve's apartment is in Seattle.
4. The students' tests are on the desk.
5. The teacher's book is in her bag.
6. Our daughters' husbands are very nice.
7. The children's room is on the second floor.
8. My friend's grandchildren visit her every weekend.

4

2. Who is wearing Mara's jacket?
3. That is not Sam's house.
4. The baby is not sleeping.
5. *Not possible to change.*
6. Amanda is here.
7. It is Jessica's car.

1. A: Does my ~~mother~~ *mother's* jacket look good on me?

   B: Hmm. I'm not sure.

2. A: The ~~women~~ *women's* restroom is over there.

   B: Thanks.

3. A: Who's ~~this~~ *that* over there?

   B: That's Ken.

4. A: Does Ken usually wear ties?

   B: No. He's wearing his ~~brother~~ *brother's* tie. And ~~this~~ *that* isn't Ken's sports jacket either.

5. A: Those earrings look really good on Judy.

   B: Yeah. I like ~~these~~ *those* earrings too.

2. parents	**6.** those	**10.** No kidding
3. parents'	**7.** roommate's	**11.** Kathy's
4. brother's	**8.** yours	**12.** love
5. these	**9.** that	

UNIT 18 (pages 83–87)

2. a	**8.** some	**14.** an	**20.** some
3. some	**9.** a	**15.** a	**21.** a
4. some	**10.** some	**16.** some	**22.** some
5. a	**11.** some	**17.** some	**23.** some
6. some	**12.** some	**18.** a	**24.** some
7. an	**13.** an	**19.** some	

2. any	**5.** some	**7.** some
3. any	**6.** some	**8.** any
4. some		

Crossed out words:

2. bowl	**4.** cup
3. a bottle of	**5.** a glass of

2. Fruit is good for you.

3. Are there any eggs for breakfast?

4. The ice cream is delicious.

5. Is the food at that restaurant good?

6. There is some bread.

7. Is there any milk?

8. These olives are salty.

3. any	**7.** any	**10.** some
4. a	**8.** an	**11.** any
5. an	**9.** a	**12.** some
6. some		

JUDY: Excuse me, waiter? Hi. Can I have ~~some~~ *a* glass of water, please?

WAITER: Sure. Ma'am, do you want mineral or regular?

JUDY: Regular, please.
[Minutes later]

WAITER: Here is your water. Are you ready to order?

JUDY: Yes. I'd like *a* sandwich and a bowl of soup. Oh, and ~~some~~ *a* small piece of chocolate cake too.

WAITER: And you, sir?

JOSH: Well, I'm not sure. ~~Are~~ *Is* the spaghetti here good?

WAITER: Yes, it's delicious.

JOSH: OK. I'd like ~~any~~ *some / Ø* spaghetti. And *a* bowl of ice cream.

WAITER: And what about something to drink?

JOSH: I want ~~the~~ *some* water. Mineral water, please.

2. cup	**6.** on	**10.** an
3. all	**7.** bowl	**11.** strawberries
4. any	**8.** some	**12.** glass
5. at	**9.** fruit	

UNIT 19 (pages 88–92)

1

2. e   **4.** c   **6.** a
3. b   **5.** d

2

Answers will vary.
  2. formal ones OR casual ones
  3. expensive ones OR cheap ones
  4. big one OR small one
  5. bright one OR dull one

3

2. a   **6.** the   **10.** the
3. a   **7.** The   **11.** an
4. the   **8.** a
5. a   **9.** the

4

3. Ø   **7.** Ø   **11.** a
4. Ø   **8.** The   **12.** an
5. Ø   **9.** a
6. The   **10.** a

5

  1. A: Try on the green jacket.
     B: But I prefer the brown ~~.~~ *one*.
  2. A: What's your favorite food?
     B: I like ~~the~~ Chinese food.
  3. A: Do you wear your black slacks to school?
     B: No, I usually wear my gray ~~one~~ *ones*.
  4. A: Do you wear ~~the~~ *a* tie to work?
     B: No, I don't like ~~the~~ ties.
  5. A: Do you have ~~an~~ *a* white dress that I could try on?
     B: Yes, I do. Here's a small one and here's a large one.
  6. A: Do you want ~~a~~ *an* umbrella?
     B: No, I never use ~~the~~ umbrellas.

6

2. a   **5.** sale   **8.** on   **11.** ones
3. an   **6.** size   **9.** look   **12.** up
4. in   **7.** the   **10.** one

UNIT 20 (pages 93–96)

1

2. can't   **4.** can   **6.** can't   **8.** can
3. can't   **5.** can   **7.** can't

2

  2. Can you give Kathy this message, please?
  3. Can you tell me the answers, please?
  4. Can you call the police, please?
  5. Can you wait for me, please?
  6. Can you help me with my homework, please?

3

  3. can't water ski / can ice skate
  4. can't play the guitar / can't play the piano
  5. can swim / can play tennis
  6. can swim / can't play tennis
  7. can't water ski / can't ice skate
  8. can play the guitar / can't play the piano
  9. *Answers will vary.*
10. *Answers will vary.*

4

  2. A: Can you speak French?
     B: No, I can't.
  3. A: Can Mike play the piano?
     B: No, he can't.
  4. A: Can Rosie understand Italian?
     B: No, she can't.
  5. A: Can the doctor see me tomorrow?
     B: Yes, he can. OR Yes, she can.
  6. A: Can you go shopping with me today?
     B: No, I can't.

5

Answers to questions will vary.
  2. How can I learn your language?   Study it.
  3. Who can cut my hair?   A hairstylist can.
  4. Where can I buy CDs?   At the music store.
  5. What can I do on the weekend in your town?   You can go dancing.

6

A: I have a problem. ~~You can~~ *Can you* help me?

B: Sure. How ~~do~~ can I help?

A: I can't ~~not~~ understand the homework. Can you understand it?

B: Yes, I ~~do~~ *can*. But I can't ~~to~~ explain it well. ~~Cans~~ *Can* the teacher explain it to you?

A: I can't ~~to~~ find him.

B: He's in his office. I'm sure he can ~~helps~~ *help* you.

UNIT 21 (pages 97–100)

1

Answers will vary.

2

2. watched	**5.** visited
3. listened	**6.** played
4. baked	

3

3. arrived	**7.** called
4. didn't cook	**8.** asked
5. enjoyed	**9.** didn't want
6. studied	**10.** didn't buy

4

2. ago	**5.** ago	**8.** yesterday
3. yesterday	**6.** yesterday	**9.** ago
4. last	**7.** last	**10.** last

5

2. didn't watch	**5.** didn't play
3. didn't talk	**6.** didn't learn
4. didn't enjoy	

6

2. /d/	**6.** /t/	**10.** /d/	**14.** /d/
3. /ɪd/	**7.** /d/	**11.** /ɪd/	**15.** /ɪd/
4. /t/	**8.** /t/	**12.** /t/	
5. /ɪd/	**9.** /d/	**13.** /ɪd/	

7

Thanks for dinner last week. I ~~enjoy~~ *enjoyed* it very much. I hope I ~~not~~ *didn't* talk too much. I ~~was~~ liked your kids a lot. Jeremy ~~did show~~ *showed* me some great computer games.

I talked to Rita's secretary again yesterday, but Rita didn't ~~returned~~ *return* my call.
—Herb

P.S. Sorry I didn't ~~thanked~~ *thank* you before, but I was very busy.

UNIT 22 (pages 101–105)

1

Base form of verb	Regular verb	Irregular verb
3. come		✓
4. leave		✓
5. see		✓
6. play	✓	
7. enjoy	✓	
8. be		✓
9. eat		✓
10. like	✓	
11. talk	✓	
12. have		✓
13. end	✓	
14. get		✓

2

2. took OR didn't take
3. slept OR didn't sleep
4. came OR didn't come
5. bought OR didn't buy
6. went OR didn't go

3

2. Sarah ate lunch today.
3. Matthew read the paper this morning. OR Matthew read the paper today.
4. Yoshi slept eight hours last night.
5. Jay and Diego went to the library yesterday.
6. I went to work last Saturday.

4

2. Henry didn't go to bed at 8:00.
3. Maria didn't buy breakfast at school.
4. John and Mary didn't read the paper.
5. Linda didn't get up at 6:00.

5

2. A: Did the teacher drink coffee in class last week?
  B: Yes, he did. OR Yes, she did.
3. A: Did you and your friends go out last week?
  B: No, we didn't.
4. A: Did Robert eat breakfast today?
  B: No, he didn't.
5. A: Did Zai and Jeffrey take the bus today?
  B: Yes, they did.
6. A: Did your friends come to your home last week?
  B: No, they didn't.
7. A: Did your friends buy ice cream today?
  B: Yes, they did.

6

1. A: ~~You did~~ *Did you* sleep well last night?
  B: No, I ~~wasn't~~ *didn't*.
2. A: I ~~go~~ *went* on a picnic last Saturday.
  B: Did you have fun?
3. A: Did you eat anything at the party last night?
  B: No, and I ~~not~~ *didn't* drink anything either.
4. A: I didn't ~~saw~~ *see* my keys on the table.
  B: We ~~putted~~ *put* them in your bag.
5. A: Did you ~~went~~ *go* to school yesterday?
  B: Yes, I went to school.

7

2. called
3. went
4. snow
5. you
6. Did
7. ate
8. drank
9. Was
10. didn't
11. happened
12. you're

UNIT 23 (pages 106–110)

1

2. a
3. e
4. f
5. c
6. b

2

2. did not stop
3. did not see
4. hit
5. got
6. had
7. stopped
8. saw
9. called
10. came

3

Answers will vary. Possible answers include:
2. When did the accident happen?
3. Who didn't stop (at the red light)?
4. Who hit the BMW?
5. Which driver got out of his car? OR Who got out of his car?
6. What did they have? OR What did the two drivers have?
7. Who stopped the fight?
8. Who called the police?

4

2. you weren't
3. did you go
4. We went
5. Did you stay
6. We spent
7. We flew
8. did you do
9. we stayed
10. talked
11. did you talk
12. I learned
13. Mark did
14. Did you meet
15. they had
16. came
17. did you meet OR you met
18. Was it
19. I enjoyed

5

1. A: What ~~had we~~ *did we have* for homework?
  B: Pages 90 and 91.
2. A: Who ~~did build~~ *built* your house?
  B: My grandfather ~~builded~~ *built* it.
3. A: Why did you ~~got~~ *get* a letter from Steven Spielberg?
  B: Because I ~~writed~~ *wrote* him and he answered my letter.

4. A: What happened at the game?

B: The other team ~~win~~ *won*.

5. A: What time *did* the game ~~began~~ *begin*?

B: It began late, at 2:30, because it rained.

6. A: How ~~the party was~~ *was the party*?

B: Oh, we had a great time.

6

2. did	**8.** broke
3. happen	**9.** dented
4. Why	**10.** What's worse
5. happened	**11.** auto repair shop
6. accident	**12.** What do you mean
7. took	

UNIT 24 (pages 111–115)

1

B: Hmm. What does she like?
A: Well, she likes sports.
B: How about a tennis racket?
A: They are too expensive.
B: Then why don't you get her a gift card?
A: That's a good idea. I'll get her a gift card at a sporting goods store! Thanks!
B: Happy to help you.

2

2. He needs a gift idea.
3. We want to go to the party.
4. It is not an appropriate gift.
5. He likes nuts and chocolate.
6. She didn't go to the party.

3

2. Kathy drove it to the party.
3. I talked to them.
4. I didn't see them.
5. Bill loves it.
6. Bill talked to us.

4

2. him	**5.** it	**8.** us
3. you / me	**6.** her	
4. you OR it / it	**7.** them	

5

2. them / they / She	**6.** you / you / he
3. him / he	**7.** her / she
4. it / me	**8.** us / them
5. it / It	

6

Dear Anne,

Thank you for inviting ~~we~~ *us* to the party. The children and ~~me~~ *I* had a great time. The games were great. The kids loved ~~they~~ *them*.

Did Bob and Sally find the gifts? I left ~~it~~ *them* in their room. Did Bob like the tennis racket? I bought it at Central Sports for ~~he~~ *him*. I got Sally's soccer ball there too. Does ~~her~~ *she* still play soccer? (I know you said "No gifts," but what's a birthday without gifts?)

Why don't ~~us~~ *we* meet one day for lunch? Give ~~I~~ *me* a call.

Talk to you soon,
Sarah

7

2. him	**6.** her	**10.** us
3. so	**7.** your	**11.** me
4. to	**8.** them	**12.** you
5. He	**9.** I	

UNIT 25 (pages 116–120)

1

Answers will vary. Possible answers include:
1. A lot. OR Not many.
2. A lot. OR Not much.
3. None. OR Not many. OR A lot.
4. A lot. OR Not many. OR None.
5. A lot. OR Not many.
6. A lot. OR Not many.
7. A lot. OR Not much. OR None.
8. A lot. OR Not many. OR None.
9. A lot. OR Not much. OR None.

2

B: It was OK.
A: How much did you eat?
B: Just a little, because the food wasn't great. But the prices were good.
A: Really? How much did you spend?
B: Not much—only $30 for all of us.
A: How many people were there?
B: Four of us.

3

2. c	4. c	6. b	8. c
3. b	5. c	7. a	

4

2. How many oranges does Steve have? — Not many.
3. How many bananas does Steve have? — Not many.
4. How much milk does Steve have? — A lot.
5. How many apples does Steve have? — A lot.
6. How much soda does Steve have? — Not much.
7. How much yogurt does Steve have? — Not much.
8. How much juice does Steve have? — A lot.
9. How many eggs does Steve have? — Not many.
10. How much food does Steve have? — Not much.

5

A: How ~~many~~ _much_ time do you get for vacation?
B: Four weeks.
A: Do you spend ^_a_ lot of time at home during your vacation?
B: No, only a ~~little~~ _few_ days.
A: Where do you usually go?
B: We spend a ~~few~~ _little_ time at my wife's parents' home. Then we go to the beach. We spend some time with our friends there.

A: How many ~~friend~~ _friends_ do you see at the beach?
B: Not ~~much~~ _many_. Four or five.

6

2. many	6. was	10. did
3. were	7. a	11. Don't ask
4. time	8. people	12. nothing
5. much	9. bet	

UNIT 26 (pages 121–125)

1

3. are	7. aren't	11. isn't
4. aren't	8. are	12. 's
5. isn't OR 's not	9. 's	
6. 's	10. are	

2

Answers will vary. Possible answers include:
2. There is a gym in my neighborhood. OR There isn't a gym in my neighborhood.
3. There is a post office in my neighborhood. OR There isn't a post office in my neighborhood.
4. There is a library in my neighborhood. OR There isn't a library in my neighborhood.
5. There are many stores in my neighborhood. OR There aren't many stores in my neighborhood.
6. There is a park in my neighborhood. OR There isn't a park in my neighborhood.
7. There is a bank in my neighborhood. OR There isn't a bank in my neighborhood.
8. There are some movie theaters in my neighborhood. OR There aren't any movie theaters in my neighborhood.
9. There are many restaurants in my neighborhood. OR There aren't many restaurants in my neighborhood.

3

2. Are there any banks on this block?
3. Is there a drugstore near here?
4. Are there any theaters in this area?
5. How many museums are there in this area?
6. Are there any buses we can take there?
7. Are there any good restaurants near the theater?
8. Is there a good place to buy art in town? OR Is there a good place in town to buy art?

4

2. there are	**8.** There isn't
3. Are there	**9.** Is there
4. there aren't	**10.** There is
5. Is there	**11.** Is there
6. there is	**12.** There is
7. Is there	

5

Hi, Rob! Greetings from Prague! We are having a great time here. Our hotel is very nice; ~~there's~~ *it's* a comfortable, reasonable place that is close to everything we want to see.

There's *are* many things to see and do here. ~~They~~ *There* is a fantastic museum not very far from our room. We went to Old Town today. ~~It's~~ *There's* an unusual clock there. It is so interesting! There ~~are~~ *is* also a very old pub there. I think it's from the 1400s. Some people were dancing there.

Let's see . . . ~~are~~ *is* there anything else I want to tell you? Oh, yes! We crossed a very beautiful, old, scary bridge yesterday. On the other side, ~~it~~ *there* was a castle! It's so amazing to be here. This place has a long, rich history.

I have to go now. We're going to see a movie tonight so we can relax. Say hi to everyone for me.
Love,
Alison

6

2. Are there	**6.** hold	**10.** snack bar
3. there's	**7.** That's	**11.** Is there
4. They're	**8.** Underground	**12.** pleasure
5. There are	**9.** restaurants	

UNIT 27 (pages 126–129)

1

2. fun / romantic	**7.** artistic
3. spy	**8.** lively / interesting
4. computer science	**9.** new / winter
5. easygoing	**10.** exciting
6. excellent / soccer	

2

Answers will vary.

3

2. Venus and Serena Williams are famous tennis players.
3. Jessica and Tim live in a big house.
4. Josh and Amanda ate at an awful restaurant.
5. Judy likes sad movies.
6. Buy this cool CD player.
7. Jeremy bought an expensive CD player.
8. Bill and Mark have important jobs.

4

2. They are interesting men.
3. The black dogs are friendly.
4. The expensive cars are over there.
5. The artistic students are young Italians.
6. The boring books have red covers.
7. The good-looking actors are from China.

5

Sentences may vary. Possible sentences include:
2. Beijing and Mexico City are big cities.
3. Ferraris and BMWs are expensive cars.
4. Prince Harry and Prince William are young men.
5. Quebec is a beautiful place.
6. Sushi is a Japanese food.
7. The Beatles were British singers.
8. The Bible is an old book.
9. Van Gogh was a poor artist.

6

A: Where were you last night?
B: I had a date.
A: Really?
B: Yeah. I met *a* beautiful woman through a personal ad.
A: Oh, yeah? Tell me about her. Is she ~~an~~ athletic like you?
B: Yeah. She plays three ~~differents~~ *different* sports.
A: What else?
B: Well, she's a ~~person~~ very funny *person*, and she listens to ~~olds~~ *old* songs like I do.

A: Does she work?

B: Yeah. She has *an* ~~a~~ interesting job with a music company.

A: She sounds like she's the *perfect* woman ~~perfect~~ for you.

B: She is.

UNIT 28 (pages 130–133)

1

One syllable: cold, dark, old, short, warm
Two syllables, ending in -*y*: busy, friendly, funny, healthy
Two syllables, not ending in -*y*: boring, honest
More than two syllables: artistic, difficult, exciting, expensive, important, interesting

2

2. funnier
3. quicker
4. worse
5. more famous
6. better
7. more important
8. more expensive
9. heavier
10. hotter

3

2. busier
3. more difficult
4. shorter
5. funnier
6. better
7. more boring
8. more active
9. worse
10. colder

4

2. more important than
3. quicker than
4. older than
5. warmer than
6. more crowded than
7. smaller than
8. worse than
9. cheaper than
10. friendlier than

5

2. Which is easier, swimming or water skiing?   *(Answers will vary.)*

3. Which are faster, planes or trains?   Planes.

4. Which is warmer, India or Russia?   India.

5. Which is more popular around the world, soccer or baseball?   Soccer.

6. Which is healthier, cake or fruit?   Fruit.

6

A: So how's your new apartment? Is it *better* ~~more good~~ than your old one?

B: Yes, it is. It's *bigger* ~~biger~~ and ~~more cheap~~ *cheaper*.

A: And where is it? Is the location good?

B: Oh, yeah. It's near the train station, so it's *easier* ~~more easy~~ for me to get to work. And I like the neighborhood too. It has a lot of trees and is ~~beautifuler~~ *more beautiful*. It's also ~~more~~ cleaner.

A: How many bedrooms are there in your apartment?

B: Well, there are three bedrooms. One bedroom is smaller ~~from~~ *than* the other two. It's ~~noisyer~~ *noisier* too. But the rest of the apartment is perfect. Why don't you come and see it this weekend?

A: That sounds like a good idea.

7

2. got
3. real
4. worse
5. better
6. older
7. food
8. than
9. cheaper
10. entertainment
11. of
12. more

UNIT 29 (pages 134–138)

1

	Adjective	Comparative	Superlative
2.	fast	*faster*	*fastest*
3.	*difficult*	more difficult	*most difficult*
4.	*scary*	*scarier*	scariest
5.	hot	*hotter*	hottest
6.	*rich*	richer	richest
7.	*friendly*	*friendlier*	friendliest
8.	important	*more important*	*most important*
9.	kind	kinder	kindest
10.	*bad*	worse	worst
11.	easy	easier	*easiest*
12.	*strange*	stranger	*strangest*
13.	*funny*	funnier	funniest
14.	good	*better*	*best*

15. *smart*	smarter	*smartest*
16. *warm*	*warmer*	warmest
17. interesting	*more interesting*	*most interesting*
18. *dangerous*	more dangerous	*most dangerous*
19. *delicious*	*more delicious*	most delicious

2

2. The MINI Cooper is the smallest car.
3. The Lincoln Navigator is the largest car.
4. Quebec is the coldest city.
5. New York is the biggest city.
6. Istanbul is the oldest city.
7. The lion is the most dangerous animal.
8. The cheetah is the fastest animal.
9. The elephant is the heaviest animal.

Answers for 10–12 may vary. Possible answers include:

10. The mystery is the most exciting book.
11. The novel is the most romantic book.
12. The textbook is the most boring book.

3

2. easier than	**7.** the worst
3. the best	**8.** the coldest
4. the most interesting	**9.** more important than
5. the largest	**10.** The fastest
6. warmer than	

4

KATHY: Did you guys buy anything nice on the trip?

AMANDA: Well, Josh bought a new stamp for his collection. And I found these three blouses in an open-air market. This pink one was ^the cheapest one I saw, and it was also ~~prettier~~ *the prettiest* one.

KATHY: Yeah, it is pretty. Actually, I think that red one is the ~~beautifulest~~ *most beautiful*.

AMANDA: Really? It was also the ^*most* expensive one they had.

KATHY: Oh, wait! This white one is really beautiful too! Hmm, it's also the ~~bigger~~ *the biggest* one. It looks too big for you.

AMANDA: You're right. I bought that one for you. I had to bring something home for ^*my* best friend!

KATHY: Oh, Amanda! That's so kind of you. I love it. Thanks!

AMANDA: You're welcome.

5

2. most exciting	**8.** terrible
3. great	**9.** scariest
4. most interesting	**10.** dangerous
5. worst	**11.** honking
6. hottest	**12.** turned out
7. rained	

UNIT 30 (pages 139–142)

1

2. at	**6.** in	**10.** in	**14.** at
3. on	**7.** in	**11.** at	**15.** on
4. on	**8.** on	**12.** at	
5. in	**9.** in	**13.** on	

2

Answers will vary. Possible answers include:

2. I go to bed at 11:00 (at night).
3. I was born in 1985.
4. I was born in June.
5. My birthday is May 15th.
6. They got married on May 18, 1980.
7. It starts at 9:00 and ends at 11:00.
8. I have English class on Mondays, Wednesdays, and Fridays.

3

2. on	**7.** on	**12.** at
3. on	**8.** at	**13.** at
4. on	**9.** in	**14.** at
5. on	**10.** at	
6. on	**11.** in	

4

Answers will vary. Possible answers include:

2. on Tuesdays and Fridays
3. on the weekends
4. on Thursday, the 3rd
5. on the 25th
6. on / November 17th
7. in
8. in
9. in the evening
10. on Friday, the 18th

5

1. A: When does class start?
   B: ~~On~~ *At* 2:00.

2. A: Is your birthday ~~on~~ *in* May?
   B: Yes, it is. It's on May 20th.

3. A: Do you ever work at ~~the~~ night?
   B: Sometimes. But I usually work in *the* morning.

4. A: When is your flight?
   B: It's ~~in~~ *at* 5:00 ~~at~~ *in* the morning.

5. A: What do you do ~~in~~ *on* weekends?
   B: ~~In~~ *On* Sundays I go to my grandparents' home for dinner.

6

2. in	**6.** afternoon	**10.** yourselves
3. doing	**7.** back	**11.** looking
4. fun	**8.** on	**12.** at
5. Saturday	**9.** two-story	

UNIT 31 (pages 143–147)

1

2. b	**4.** b	**6.** b
3. a	**5.** a	

2

2. [They're] going to see a movie.
3. [He's] going to sleep.
4. [They're] going to have lunch.
5. [He's] going to buy some food.
6. [She's] going to teach.
7. [He's] going to exercise.
8. [They're] going to have a party.

3

2. isn't going to spend OR 's not going to spend
3. aren't going to watch
4. isn't going to teach
5. aren't going to visit
6. isn't going to take OR 's not going to take

4

2. I'm going to eat out. OR I'm not going to eat out.
3. I'm going to go out with friends. OR I'm not going to go out with friends.
4. I'm going to go shopping. OR I'm not going to go shopping.
5. I'm going to go to the movies. OR I'm not going to go to the movies.
6. I'm going to play soccer. OR I'm not going to play soccer.
7. I'm going to study. OR I'm not going to study.
8. I'm going to visit relatives. OR I'm not going to visit relatives.
9. I'm going to wake up early. OR I'm not going to wake up early.
10. I'm going to work. OR I'm not going to work.

5

I can't believe the course is almost over. ~~It~~ *It's* going to end in one week. Most of my classmates are going *to* return home, but some are ~~no~~ *not* going to leave. Rana *is* going to start a new job. Misha is going to ~~taking~~ *take* another course. Masao and Laura ~~is~~ *are* going to get married, and I'm going to go to their wedding.

6

2. hurry	**6.** doing	**10.** start
3. going	**7.** come	**11.** chill
4. not	**8.** have	**12.** to
5. faster	**9.** jam	

UNIT 32 (pages 148–151)

1

2. f	**4.** a	**6.** c	**8.** d
3. h	**5.** g	**7.** b	

2

2. Yes, I am. OR No, I'm not.
3. Yes, I am. OR No, I'm not.
4. Yes, I am. OR No, I'm not.
5. Yes, I am. OR No, I'm not.
6. Yes, I am. OR No, I'm not.
7. Yes, I am. OR No, I'm not.
8. Yes, I am. OR No, I'm not.

3

2. in two years
3. in three months
4. next month
5. in five days
6. next year

4

2. A: Is Mrs. Olson going to take the job?
  B: Yes, she is.
3. A: Are you and your classmates going to study tomorrow?
  B: No, we aren't. OR No, we're not.
4. A: Are Josh's parents going to move next year?
  B: Yes, they are.
5. A: Is Tim going to get a haircut?
  B: Yes, he is.
6. A: Are you going to stay in bed today?
  B: No, I'm not.

5

MARY: Hi, Annie. It's Grandma. How are you?

ANNIE: OK. Grandma, are you going ^to^ visit us this weekend?

MARY: No, I'm not going. ~~I~~ ^to I'm^ going to visit Uncle Steve.

ANNIE: ^Is^ Grandpa going to go with you?

MARY: Yes, ~~he's~~ ^he is^. Why?

ANNIE: Because I'm bored. Mom is always at work, and we never do anything fun.

MARY: Let me talk to your mother.

ANNIE: She isn't here. She ^is^ going ~~being~~ ^to be^ late tonight. Do you want to talk to Jeremy?

MARY: Why? Where's your dad? ~~He is~~ ^Is he^ going to be late tonight too?

ANNIE: Yeah. They're both going to come home late.

MARY: Well, don't worry. I'm ~~go~~ ^going^ to talk to both of them.

6

2. Not bad
3. was
4. Actually
5. It's
6. Are
7. matter of fact
8. be
9. Is
10. going
11. I'm
12. isn't

UNIT 33 (pages 152–156)

1

2. Who
3. When
4. What
5. How
6. Who
7. Why
8. Where

2

2. Who is going to get a ticket? — The owner of the car.
3. Who is going to take something from the old woman? — The man in the black shirt.
4. What is the man in the black shirt going to take? — The woman's wallet.
5. How is the old woman going to feel? — Angry.
6. Where is the owner of the car going to go? — On a ski vacation.
7. Why are the people going to go into the movie theater? — Because they're going to see a movie.
8. When is the movie going to start? — At 5:00.

3

Answers will vary.

4

2. Who are they going to invite?
3. What are you going to buy?
4. How are you going to get there?
5. Where is she going to go?
6. When are you going to clean it?

5

A: Did you hear the news? Amanda's pregnant.

B: Really? When ~~she is~~ *is she* going to have the baby?

A: At the end of January. She's going to ~~stopping work~~ *stop working* in the middle of December.

B: Are we going *to* have a party for her?

A: Yes. We *are* going to have it in early December.

B: Wow, Amanda and her husband are *going* to have a baby!

A: *It's* ~~It~~ going to be very exciting for them.

B: What ~~is~~ *are* she and Josh going to name the baby?

A: I have no idea.

B: Where *are* they going to live? Their apartment is very small.

A: I think they're going to move.

6

2. How
3. say
4. You're
5. marry
6. took
7. What
8. are
9. have
10. yeah
11. engaged
12. Congratulations

Test: Units 1–2

PART ONE

DIRECTIONS: Circle the letter of the correct answer to complete each sentence.

Example

_____ right at the corner.   A B Ⓒ D

(A) Is turn   (C) Turn
(B) Turns   (D) Turn not

1. A: Can I park here?   A B C D
   B: No, _____ here.

   (A) is park   (C) not park
   (B) don't park   (D) parking

2. A: _____ your classmates?   A B C D
   B: Yes, they are.

   (A) Are these   (C) This is
   (B) Is this   (D) These is

3. _____ me.   A B C D

   (A) Helping   (C) Please help
   (B) Help please   (D) Helps

4. A: _____ my friend Jack.   A B C D
   B: Nice to meet you, Jack.

   (A) This is   (C) He
   (B) It is   (D) Is

5. Please _____ the door.   A B C D

   (A) opening   (C) opens
   (B) open   (D) no open

6. Jean and I are on time. _____ are not late.   A B C D

   (A) We   (C) Us
   (B) They   (D) I

7. A: _____ a good restaurant?   A B C D
   B: Yes, it is.

   (A) This is   (C) Isn't
   (B) Is this   (D) Is

(continued)

8. _____ smoke here.   A B C D

   (A) Don't   (C) Not
   (B) Doesn't   (D) No

9. _____ is a good book.   A B C D

   (A) He   (C) Was
   (B) It's   (D) It

10. _____ the question, please.   A B C D

   (A) Is answer   (C) Answers
   (B) Answering   (D) Answer

11. My father is a teacher. _____ isn't a writer.   A B C D

   (A) She   (C) It
   (B) He   (D) He no

12. _____ to the CD.   A B C D

   (A) Is listen   (C) Listens
   (B) Do listens   (D) Listen

PART TWO

DIRECTIONS: Each sentence has four underlined words or phrases. The four underlined parts of the sentence are marked A, B, C, and D. Circle the letter of the <u>one</u> underlined word or phrase that is NOT CORRECT.

Example
<u>These</u> <u>are</u> <u>my</u> <u>friend</u> Mark and Ben.   A B C Ⓓ
  A   B   C   D

13. <u>Stops</u> <u>at</u> the <u>bus</u> stop, <u>please</u>.   A B C D
   A   B   C   D

14. <u>These</u> <u>is</u> <u>my</u> <u>brother</u>, George.   A B C D
   A   B C   D

15. <u>Take it</u> <u>the</u> <u>bus</u> across <u>town</u>.   A B C D
   A   B   C   D

16. My <u>classes</u> <u>are</u> good, but <u>it</u> <u>are</u> hard.   A B C D
      A   B   C D

17. <u>Going</u> two <u>blocks</u> and <u>turn</u> <u>left</u>.   A B C D
   A   B   C   D

18. <u>Please</u> <u>closes</u> <u>the</u> <u>window</u>.   A B C D
   A   B   C   D

19. <u>The glass</u> <u>it is</u> <u>full</u> of <u>water</u>.   A B C D
   A   B   C   D

20. <u>Do</u> <u>no</u> <u>open</u> the door, <u>please</u>.   A B C D
   A   B   C   D

Test: Units 3–6

PART ONE

DIRECTIONS: Circle the letter of the correct answer to complete each sentence.

Example
I _____ a teacher.   Ⓐ B C D

(A) am   (C) are
(B) be   (D) is

1. A: Where's your new apartment?   A B C D
   - B: It's _____ Washington Avenue.

   (A) at   (C) across
   (B) in   (D) on

2. _____ a very good Indian restaurant.   A B C D

   (A) Is that   (C) Those are
   (B) That is   (D) Are those

3. She _____ from London.   A B C D

   (A) isn't   (C) no is
   (B) is no   (D) 's isn't

4. A: _____ this your apartment building?   A B C D
   B: Yes, it is.

   (A) Are   (C) It
   (B) It is   (D) Is

5. A: _____'s the library?   A B C D
   B: It's at 52 Cleveland Avenue.

   (A) When   (C) Who
   (B) Where   (D) What

6. A: _____ your friends?   A B C D
   B: Yes, they are.

   (A) Those aren't   (C) That is
   (B) Are those   (D) Is that

7. _____ married. They're friends.   A B C D

   (A) They aren't   (C) They not
   (B) They isn't   (D) Aren't they

(continued)

8. A: _____ is that man?
   B: He's my father.   A B C D

   (**A**) What   (**C**) Who
   (**B**) Why   (**D**) How

9. _____ an old woman.   A B C D

   (**A**) She   (**C**) We're
   (**B**) She's   (**D**) You

10. Those are _____ students. I teach them English.   A B C D

    (**A**) its   (**C**) a
    (**B**) our   (**D**) my

11. _____ you and Mark friends?   A B C D

    (**A**) Are   (**C**) What
    (**B**) Is   (**D**) Are no

12. They are _____ 10th floor.   A B C D

    (**A**) at the   (**C**) on the
    (**B**) in the   (**D**) on

PART TWO

DIRECTIONS: Each sentence has four underlined words or phrases. The four underlined parts of the sentence are marked A, B, C, and D. Circle the letter of the one underlined word or phrase that is NOT CORRECT.

Example
Is you a reporter?   Ⓐ B C D
 A   B C   D
13. The childs are on the third floor.   A B C D
       A   B   C   D
14. They are no from New York.   A B C D
     A   B   C   D
15. What the name of that restaurant?   A B C D
     A   B   C   D
16. My apartment is across the bank.   A B C D
     A   B   C   D
17. The peoples are from Australia.   A B C D
        A   B   C   D
18. Who that woman standing by Julia?   A B C D
     A   B   C   D
19. We be not from Turkey.   A B C D
     A B   C   D
20. The school is next the library.   A B C D
        A   B   C   D

Test: Units 7–8

PART ONE

DIRECTIONS: Circle the letter of the correct answer to complete each sentence.

Example
Tom _____ at the concert last night.　　　　　　　　　　A Ⓑ C D

(A) is　　　　　　　　　(C) were
(B) was　　　　　　　　(D) isn't

1. A: How was the weather?　　　　　　　　　　　　　A B C D
   B: _____ was cold and rainy.

   (A) She　　　　　　　　(C) We
   (B) What　　　　　　　(D) It

2. She _____ at home last night.　　　　　　　　　A B C D

   (A) wasn't　　　　　　(C) were
   (B) isn't　　　　　　　(D) no was

3. A: _____ were you in Paris?　　　　　　　　　　A B C D
   B: For two weeks.

   (A) Who　　　　　　　(C) How
   (B) How long　　　　　(D) When

4. Kathy and Mark _____ late for the movie.　　　A B C D

   (A) was　　　　　　　(C) wasn't
   (B) no were　　　　　(D) weren't

5. A: _____ were you?　　　　　　　　　　　　　　A B C D
   B: I was home. I was sick.

   (A) Where　　　　　　(C) Why
   (B) Was　　　　　　　(D) Who

6. A: _____ you at school yesterday?　　　　　　A B C D
   B: Yes, I was.

   (A) When　　　　　　(C) Were
   (B) Are　　　　　　　(D) Was

7. A: _____ at the game yesterday?　　　　　　　A B C D
   B: Amanda, Steve, Josh, and Jessica were there.

   (A) Who's　　　　　　(C) Where were
   (B) Who was　　　　　(D) How was

(continued)

8. A: Was Mr. James at the meeting last night?
   B: Yes, _____ .

   (**A**) they was   (**C**) he wasn't
   (**B**) he's   (**D**) he was

   A   B   C   D

9. A: _____ your test this morning?
   B: It wasn't bad.

   (**A**) How were   (**C**) What was
   (**B**) How was   (**D**) Where was

   A   B   C   D

10. My friends _____ not at the game yesterday.

    (**A**) are   (**C**) were
    (**B**) wasn't   (**D**) we're

    A   B   C   D

11. A: _____ Mark with last night?
    B: Amanda.

    (**A**) When was   (**C**) How was
    (**B**) Who was   (**D**) What was

    A   B   C   D

12. A: Were you home last night?
    B: No, _____ .

    (**A**) you weren't   (**C**) I wasn't
    (**B**) we were   (**D**) we wasn't

    A   B   C   D

PART TWO

DIRECTIONS: Each sentence has four underlined words or phrases. The four underlined parts of the sentence are marked A, B, C, and D. Circle the letter of the one underlined word or phrase that is NOT CORRECT.

Example
Lucy, we <u>was</u> <u>at</u> <u>your house</u> <u>last night</u>.
      A   B   C   D

(Ⓐ) B   C   D

13. <u>How long</u> <u>was</u> you <u>on vacation</u> with <u>your family</u>?
     A   B   C   D

A   B   C   D

14. <u>Was</u> David and Jean <u>at</u> <u>the party</u> <u>last night</u>?
    A   B   C   D

A   B   C   D

15. <u>How</u> <u>were</u> <u>the weather</u> on <u>your trip</u>?
    A   B   C   D

A   B   C   D

16. <u>The</u> <u>movie</u> <u>no was</u> <u>good</u>.
    A   B   C   D

A   B   C   D

17. <u>Where</u> <u>was</u> <u>it</u> <u>the</u> movie?
     A   B   C   D

A   B   C   D

18. <u>My parents</u> <u>wasn't</u> <u>happy</u> <u>about the play</u>.
       A   B   C   D

A   B   C   D

19. <u>How</u> <u>long</u> <u>was</u> you <u>there</u>?
     A   B   C   D

A   B   C   D

20. <u>When</u> <u>you were</u> <u>in Italy</u> <u>on vacation</u>?
     A   B   C   D

A   B   C   D

Test: Units 9–13

PART ONE

Directions: Circle the letter of the correct answer to complete each sentence.

Example

Do you _____ a good doctor?   (Ⓐ) B   C   D

(**A**) know   (**C**) haves
(**B**) knows   (**D**) have it

1. A: Do you _____ an appointment?   A   B   C   D
   B: Yes, I do.

   (**A**) needs   (**C**) need it
   (**B**) need   (**D**) wants

2. Soo Jin _____ art class today.   A   B   C   D

   (**A**) in   (**C**) has
   (**B**) no has   (**D**) have

3. A: _____ you go to bed?   A   B   C   D
   B: Usually at 10:00.

   (**A**) Why do   (**C**) What time does
   (**B**) When does   (**D**) What time do

4. A: How often do you eat meat?   A   B   C   D
   B: _____. I don't like it.

   (**A**) Rarely   (**C**) Often
   (**B**) Always   (**D**) Usually

5. A: _____ Marley stay up late?   A   B   C   D
   B: She works and goes to school. She has a lot to do.

   (**A**) When does   (**C**) What does
   (**B**) Why does   (**D**) How long does

6. A: What does Bill look like?   A   B   C   D
   B: He _____ tall and _____ black wavy hair.

   (**A**) has, is   (**C**) is, has
   (**B**) was, got   (**D**) is, have

7. A: Do you get enough sleep?   A   B   C   D
   B: Well, I do _____, on weekends.

   (**A**) never   (**C**) always
   (**B**) rarely   (**D**) sometimes

(continued)

T-7

8. A: _____ a hairstylist?   A B C D
   B: Yes, he is.

   (**A**) It's he   (**C**) He is
   (**B**) Is he   (**D**) Is she

9. Mike _____ a very expensive car.   A B C D

   (**A**) want it   (**C**) wanting
   (**B**) want   (**D**) wants

10. A: Who _____ green eyes?   A B C D
   B: Marta does.

   (**A**) has it   (**C**) has
   (**B**) have   (**D**) have it

11. A: How _____ your new job?   A B C D
   B: I like it very much.

   (**A**) do you like   (**C**) do like
   (**B**) like you   (**D**) like it

12. I _____ 22 years old.   A B C D

   (**A**) have   (**C**) is
   (**B**) am   (**D**) be

PART TWO

DIRECTIONS: Each sentence has four underlined words or phrases. The four underlined parts of the sentence are marked A, B, C, and D. Circle the letter of the <u>one</u> underlined word or phrase that is NOT CORRECT.

Example
She eats never at expensive restaurants.   A Ⓑ C D
 A   B   C   D

13. The teacher never is late for class.   A B C D
    A   B   C D

14. Does Robert likes the new music store?   A B C D
    A   B   C   D

15. The Kims needs a new apartment.   A B C D
    A   B   C   D

16. We always are on time for the movies.   A B C D
    A   B   C   D

17. Mr. Perez is tall and is short, brown hair.   A B C D
    A   B   C   D

18. Who always does wakes up early?   A B C D
    A   B   C   D

19. Does the Thai restaurant costs a lot of money? A B C D
    A   B   C   D

20. You needs more money for lunch.   A B C D
    A   B   C   D

Test: Units 14–16

PART ONE

DIRECTIONS: Circle the letter of the correct answer to complete each sentence.

Example

She _____ right now.   A (B) C D

(A) sleeping   (C) is sleeps
(B) is sleeping   (D) are sleeping

1. A: _____ singing?   A B C D
   B: My brother is.

   (A) Who   (C) Who is
   (B) What   (D) Is that

2. A: _____ the children eating their dinner?   A B C D
   B: Yes, they are. They're having pizza.

   (A) Why are   (C) Are
   (B) Where are   (D) Is

3. He _____ fixing the car right now.   A B C D

   (A) no is   (C) no
   (B) 's not   (D) not

4. A: _____ making dinner?   A B C D
   B: I'm hungry.

   (A) Why are you   (C) When are you
   (B) When you are   (D) Where you are

5. A: _____ getting a haircut?   A B C D
   B: No, he's not.

   (A) Is he   (C) He is
   (B) Are they   (D) Are you

6. _____ watching TV at the moment.   A B C D

   (A) We're   (C) We
   (B) Are   (D) We is

7. How are you _____ the stew?   A B C D

   (A) make   (C) makes
   (B) making   (D) make it

(continued)

8. _____ raining in New York today?   A B C D

   (**A**) Is there   (**C**) Its
   (**B**) Isn't   (**D**) Is it

9. A: Is she going to the movies?   A B C D
   B: Yes, _____.

   (**A**) she's   (**C**) she's going
   (**B**) she is   (**D**) she going

10. A: _____ are the Smiths eating for dinner?   A B C D
   B: Chicken and rice.

   (**A**) Where   (**C**) How
   (**B**) Why   (**D**) What

11. A: Is he having lunch now?   A B C D
   B: _____.

   (**A**) Yes, he's   (**C**) No, not
   (**B**) Yes, he is   (**D**) No, he's isn't

12. A: What is Gerald doing now?   A B C D
   B: He's _____.

   (**A**) eating and is watching TV   (**C**) eating and watching TV
   (**B**) eats   (**D**) eats and watches TV

PART TWO

DIRECTIONS: Each sentence has four underlined words or phrases. The four underlined parts of the sentence are marked A, B, C, and D. Circle the letter of the <u>one</u> underlined word or phrase that is NOT CORRECT.

Example
They <u>are</u> <u>work</u> <u>at home</u> <u>today</u>.   A Ⓑ C D
    A   B   C   D

13. <u>My</u> cell phone <u>aren't</u> <u>working</u> <u>right now</u>.   A B C D
    A   B   C   D

14. <u>What</u> <u>you are</u> <u>doing</u> <u>right now</u>?   A B C D
    A   B   C   D

15. <u>Is</u> <u>Judy</u> <u>has</u> <u>a good time</u> on vacation?   A B C D
    A   B   C   D

16. <u>Why is</u> Martin <u>goes</u> <u>to school</u> <u>so early</u>?   A B C D
    A   B   C   D

17. <u>Who</u> <u>is it</u> <u>having</u> spaghetti for <u>lunch</u>?   A B C D
    A   B   C   D

18. <u>The flowers</u> <u>growing</u> <u>tall</u> <u>in the garden</u>.   A B C D
    A   B   C   D

19. <u>Is</u> <u>Jay</u> <u>practices</u> <u>for his concert</u>?   A B C D
    A B   C   D

20. <u>Ben's</u> <u>reading</u> and <u>is listening</u> <u>to music</u>.   A B C D
    A   B   C   D

Test: Units 17–20

PART ONE

Directions: Circle the letter of the correct answer to complete each sentence.

Example

_____ tie is very nice.   A B Ⓒ D

(A) Those   (C) That
(B) It   (D) These

1. A: Can Paul help me?   A B C D
   B: Yes, _____.

   (A) it can   (C) he can't
   (B) he can   (D) they can

2. Those _____ aren't new.   A B C D

   (A) tie   (C) shirt
   (B) sports jacket   (D) pants

3. _____ good for you.   A B C D

   (A) Rice are   (C) Rice is
   (B) A rice is   (D) Rices are

4. A: Do you like the blue shirt?   A B C D
   B: Yes, and I like the red _____ too.

   (A) the   (C) ones
   (B) one   (D) and

5. A: May I have _____ coffee?   A B C D
   B: Of course.

   (A) any   (C) a bowl of
   (B) a cup   (D) a cup of

6. A: Can you _____ me a favor, please?   A B C D
   B: Sure, what?

   (A) are   (C) do
   (B) have   (D) give

7. _____ shoes are small on me. I need some new ones.   A B C D

   (A) That   (C) This
   (B) A   (D) These

(continued)

8. My _____ car is on the street. They parked it there last night.   A B C D

   (A) parents   (C) parents'
   (B) parent's   (D) parent'

9. I like _____ juice and milk.   A B C D

   (A) an orange   (C) the orange
   (B) a orange   (D) orange

10. A: Do they have a car and a truck?   A B C D
    B: Yes, but _____ truck is at the repair shop.

    (A) a   (C) Ø
    (B) the   (D) an

11. Pablo needs to study English. He _____ any English.   A B C D

    (A) can't speak   (C) can speak
    (B) speaks   (D) can't speaks

12. A: Do you have my tie?   A B C D
    B: Do you mean _____?

    (A) a blue tie   (C) blue ones
    (B) the blue one   (D) a blue one

PART TWO

DIRECTIONS: Each sentence has four underlined words or phrases. The four underlined parts of the sentence are marked A, B, C, and D. Circle the letter of the <u>one</u> underlined word or phrase that is NOT CORRECT.

Example
You <u>have</u> <u>a</u> <u>interview</u> <u>tomorrow</u>.   A Ⓑ C D
    A B   C   D

13. <u>What</u> <u>I can</u> <u>do</u> <u>to help you</u>?   A B C D
    A   B   C   D

14. <u>The cereal</u> <u>is</u> <u>my</u> favorite breakfast <u>food</u>.   A B C D
    A   B C   D

15. <u>Those</u> <u>sports jacket</u> <u>is</u> <u>my brother's</u>.   A B C D
    A   B   C   D

16. <u>They</u> <u>are buying</u> <u>a jackets</u> for <u>the children</u>.   A B C D
    A   B   C   D

17. <u>Ben</u> <u>wants</u> <u>some</u> <u>piece</u> of toast.   A B C D
    A   B   C   D

18. <u>Are</u> <u>this</u> <u>your</u> <u>sunglasses</u>?   A B C D
    A   B   C   D

19. <u>Josh</u> <u>ordered</u> <u>a meat and rice</u> <u>at the restaurant</u>.   A B C D
    A   B   C   D

20. <u>Pedro</u> <u>can</u> <u>to read</u> <u>English newspapers</u>.   A B C D
    A   B   C   D

Test: Units 21–23

PART ONE

DIRECTIONS: Circle the letter of the correct answer to complete each sentence.

Example

We are sorry we _____ your party.   A B Ⓒ D

(**A**) miss   (**C**) missed
(**B**) did miss   (**D**) miss it

1. A: _____ happened?   A B C D
   B: He had a small accident.

   (**A**) Why   (**C**) What
   (**B**) Who   (**D**) When

2. We _____ our jackets and left.   A B C D

   (**A**) putted on   (**C**) put it
   (**B**) put on   (**D**) puts on

3. The Parkers _____ of the hotel yesterday afternoon.   A B C D

   (**A**) checks out   (**C**) check out
   (**B**) did checked out   (**D**) checked out

4. The children _____ one bedroom.   A B C D

   (**A**) slept in   (**C**) sleeped in
   (**B**) sleep on   (**D**) sleeps in

5. We _____ any coffee.   A B C D

   (**A**) drank   (**C**) drank it
   (**B**) didn't drink   (**D**) no drank

6. Where _____ happen?   A B C D

   (**A**) the accident   (**C**) the accident did
   (**B**) accident did   (**D**) did the accident

7. The guests _____ last night.   A B C D

   (**A**) leaved   (**C**) did left
   (**B**) did arrive   (**D**) arrived

(continued)

8. A: Who took the car to the auto repair shop?   A B C D
   B: _____.

   (A) Bob and I take it   (C) Bob and I doed
   (B) Bob and I did   (D) Bob and I taked it

9. You _____ your homework.   A B C D

   (A) didn't finish   (C) finished no
   (B) no finish   (D) did it finish

10. I saw your presentation yesterday. I _____ it.   A B C D

    (A) did love   (C) did loved
    (B) do love   (D) loved

11. When _____ arrive at the convention?   A B C D

    (A) did   (C) did you
    (B) you did   (D) you

12. _____ anything to eat for lunch?   A B C D

    (A) You did had   (C) Did you had
    (B) You had   (D) Did you have

PART TWO

DIRECTIONS: Each sentence has four underlined words or phrases. The four underlined parts of the sentence are marked A, B, C, and D. Circle the letter of the <u>one</u> underlined word or phrase that is NOT CORRECT.

Example
<u>We was</u> <u>at</u> <u>the presentation</u> <u>yesterday morning</u>.   (A) B C D
   A   B   C   D

13. <u>We</u> <u>did drink</u> <u>all the milk</u> <u>yesterday</u>.   A B C D
    A   B   C   D

14. <u>What</u> <u>did happened</u> <u>to you</u> <u>last night</u>?   A B C D
    A   B   C   D

15. <u>They</u> <u>didn't</u> <u>listened it</u> to the teacher <u>yesterday</u>.   A B C D
    A   B   C   D

16. <u>The baby</u> <u>born was</u> <u>during</u> <u>the night</u>.   A B C D
    A   B   C   D

17. <u>Who did</u> <u>had</u> <u>an accident</u> <u>yesterday evening</u>?   A B C D
    A   B   C   D

18. <u>Her</u> <u>parents</u> <u>not stay</u> <u>all</u> weekend.   A B C D
    A   B   C   D

19. <u>Did you</u> <u>had</u> <u>the money</u> <u>for</u> the train?   A B C D
     A   B   C   D

20. <u>What</u> <u>did</u> <u>the doctor</u> <u>said</u>?   A B C D
    A   B   C   D

Test: Units 24–26

PART ONE

DIRECTIONS: Circle the letter of the correct answer to complete each sentence.

Example

Can I give _____ to her?   (A) B   C   D

(**A**) them   (**C**) they
(**B**) she   (**D**) he

1. There _____ post office near here.   A   B   C   D

(**A**) no is   (**C**) isn't no
(**B**) isn't a   (**D**) not a

2. How _____ time did you spend there?   A   B   C   D

(**A**) much   (**C**) many
(**B**) the   (**D**) few

3. _____ knows the people very well.   A   B   C   D

(**A**) I   (**C**) They
(**B**) She   (**D**) You

4. _____ there much rain in Seattle?   A   B   C   D

(**A**) Are   (**C**) Has
(**B**) Is   (**D**) Have

5. Is it OK to _____ flowers?   A   B   C   D

(**A**) giving she   (**C**) gives hers
(**B**) her give   (**D**) give her

6. A: How many people did you meet there?   A   B   C   D
   B: _____.

(**A**) Not many   (**C**) A little
(**B**) Not much   (**D**) Much

7. A: Is there a bed and breakfast near there?   A   B   C   D
   B: No, _____.

(**A**) there is   (**C**) there isn't
(**B**) there aren't   (**D**) there no is

(continued)

8. _____ both have birthdays in July.   A B C D

   (A) There   (C) They're
   (B) Their   (D) They

9. A: _____ times did you see *Star Wars*?   A B C D
   B: A lot of times!

   (A) How much   (C) Many
   (B) A few   (D) How many

10. I want to buy _____ a gift.   A B C D

    (A) him   (C) she
    (B) he   (D) hers

11. A: _____ any nice restaurants nearby?   A B C D
    B: Yes. Try Milo's on Second Avenue.

    (A) There are   (C) Are there
    (B) Is there   (D) There's

12. A: How much _____ did you drink?   A B C D
    B: A few cups.

    (A) sodas   (C) cups of coffee
    (B) coffee   (D) the coffee

PART TWO

DIRECTIONS: Each sentence has four underlined words or phrases. The four underlined parts of the sentence are marked A, B, C, and D. Circle the letter of the one underlined word or phrase that is NOT CORRECT.

Example
Is there any nice places to eat here?   Ⓐ B C D
  A   B   C   D

13. How many time did you spend in the capital?   A B C D
    A   B   C   D

14. There is many people on the bus.   A B C D
    A   B   C   D

15. We are giving he a new toy for his birthday.   A B C D
    A   B   C   D

16. How much money it cost?   A B C D
    A   B   C D

17. There isn't no library in the town.   A B C D
    A   B   C   D

18. Jeremy knows them enjoy music.   A B C D
    A   B   C   D

19. How much brothers do you have?   A B C D
    A   B   C   D

20. Are there a non-smoking room available?   A B C D
    A   B   C   D

Test: Units 27–30

PART ONE

DIRECTIONS: Circle the letter of the correct answer to complete each sentence.

Example

He's a young _____ player.　　　　　　　　　　　Ⓐ　B　C　D

(A) baseball　　　　　(C) friendliest
(B) artist　　　　　　(D) -at-hearts

1. My brother is _____ me.　　　　　　　　　　　A　B　C　D

(A) young　　　　　　(C) young than
(B) oldest　　　　　　(D) older than

2. We met with the group _____.　　　　　　　　A　B　C　D

(A) on 9:00　　　　　(C) 9:30
(B) at 10:30　　　　　(D) in 10:00

3. Francesco's is _____ place to eat in town.　　　A　B　C　D

(A) the better　　　　(C) the best
(B) best　　　　　　　(D) the great

4. Mike likes to take _____ drives in the car.　　A　B　C　D

(A) bored　　　　　　(C) best
(B) travel　　　　　　(D) long

5. Susan goes to an _____ school.　　　　　　　A　B　C　D

(A) college　　　　　(C) high
(B) art　　　　　　　(D) great

6. A: What is the _____ movie?　　　　　　　　A　B　C　D
   B: *The Sixth Sense* is.

(A) scaryest　　　　　(C) scary
(B) scarest　　　　　(D) scariest

7. A: Is Prague the _____ city in Europe?　　　　A　B　C　D
   B: Yes, I think it is.

(A) older　　　　　　(C) more fun
(B) nicest　　　　　　(D) beautifulest

(continued)

8. Mrs. Kim's appointment is _____.   A B C D

   (A) on May   (C) in the morning
   (B) at the 10th   (D) in night

9. They sell _____ wallets at the store.   A B C D

   (A) brown leather   (C) leather brown
   (B) brown leathers   (D) a brown leather

10. James always wants to play _____.   A B C D

   (A) on dinner time   (C) at bedtime
   (B) in bedtime   (D) in dinner time

11. A: Which is better, Bombay or Laguna?   A B C D
    B: Laguna is _____.

   (A) worser   (C) more better
   (B) better and cheaper (D) the worst

12. Rome was _____ city on our trip.   A B C D

   (A) the older   (C) the most interesting
   (B) the most good   (D) a warmer

PART TWO

DIRECTIONS: Each sentence has four underlined words or phrases. The four underlined parts of the sentence are marked A, B, C, and D. Circle the letter of the <u>one</u> underlined word or phrase that is NOT CORRECT.

Example
Which is best, Rome or Milan?   A B Ⓒ D
A   B   C   D

13. It was the interesting thing that happened.   A B C D
A   B   C   D

14. The museum was interestinger than the show.   A B C D
A   B   C   D

15. The party was in Thursday, January 1st.   A B C D
A   B   C   D

16. It was coldest day of the vacation.   A B C D
A   B   C   D

17. He has a winter new jacket.   A B C D
A   B   C   D

18. My history class begins on 10:00.   A B C D
A   B   C   D

19. Which is easier than to learn, English or French?   A B C D
A   B   C   D

20. Max is a active young boy.   A B C D
A   B C   D

Test: Units 31–33

PART ONE

DIRECTIONS: Circle the letter of the correct answer to complete each sentence.

Example

_____ going to be late?   A Ⓑ C D

(A) We are   (C) Is we
(B) Are we   (D) You are

1. It's _____ to rain. It's going to be sunny.   A B C D

   (A) no is   (C) not going
   (B) going no   (D) is no going

2. _____ going to come to the soccer game?   A B C D

   (A) Is we   (C) They are
   (B) We are   (D) Are you

3. What _____ to do on Saturday?   A B C D

   (A) are you going   (C) you are having
   (B) you are going   (D) is you going

4. Is _____ a lot of work?   A B C D

   (A) the job being   (C) he going
   (B) it going to be   (D) it having to be

5. Roberto _____ more money.   A B C D

   (A) going to earn   (C) is going earn
   (B) earning   (D) is going to earn

6. A: When is he _____ the job?   A B C D
   B: In two weeks.

   (A) starts   (C) going to start
   (B) is going to start (D) is going start

7. A: When are your parents coming?   A B C D
   B: They are going _____ on Sunday.

   (A) arriving   (C) to arrive
   (B) arrive   (D) to arrives

(continued)

8. Are Joe and Maria going _____ a baby soon?   A B C D

   (A) have   (C) having
   (B) to have   (D) had

9. A: _____ are you going to go to the football game?   A B C D
   B: On Saturday at 1:00.

   (A) How   (C) When
   (B) What's   (D) Why

10. The game _____ start soon.   A B C D

    (A) isn't going to   (C) won't be going to
    (B) no going   (D) is not going

11. A: Is it going _____ tonight?   A B C D
    B: Yes, it is. Drive home slowly.

    (A) snowing   (C) snows
    (B) to snow   (D) to be snow

12. A: _____ going to buy a new car?   A B C D
    B: Mine is very old.

    (A) When are you   (C) Why are you
    (B) Why you are   (D) How are you

PART TWO

DIRECTIONS: Each sentence has four underlined words or phrases. The four underlined parts of the sentence are marked A, B, C, and D. Circle the letter of the <u>one</u> underlined word or phrase that is NOT CORRECT.

Example

<u>How</u> I <u>going</u> <u>to ask</u> you <u>this</u>?   A Ⓑ C D
  A   B   C   D

13. <u>How</u> long <u>you going</u> <u>to be</u> <u>in Spain</u>?   A B C D
    A   B   C   D

14. <u>It's no</u> <u>going to</u> <u>be cold</u> <u>tomorrow</u>.   A B C D
    A   B   C   D

15. <u>Am</u> <u>going to</u> <u>be</u> <u>on time</u> <u>for the movie</u>?   A B C D
    A   B   C   D

16. <u>When</u> <u>he is</u> <u>going to be</u> <u>home tomorrow</u>?   A B C D
    A   B   C   D

17. <u>There isn't</u> <u>going be</u> <u>much</u> <u>traffic tonight</u>.   A B C D
    A   B   C   D

18. <u>Is Jerry</u> and Sam <u>going</u> <u>to be</u> <u>in the school play</u>? A B C D
    A   B   C   D

19. <u>Does</u> <u>the game</u> <u>going</u> to start <u>at 10:00</u>?   A B C D
    A   B   C   D

20. <u>Who going</u> <u>to do</u> <u>the shopping</u> <u>this week</u>?   A B C D
    A   B   C   D

Answer Key for Tests

Correct responses for Part Two questions appear in parentheses.

UNITS 1–2

Part One

1. B	7. B
2. A	8. A
3. C	9. D
4. A	10. D
5. B	11. B
6. A	12. D

Part Two

13. A (Stop)	17. A (Go)
14. A (This)	18. B (Close)
15. A (Take)	19. B (is)
16. C (they)	20. B (not)

UNITS 3–6

Part One

1. D	7. A
2. B	8. C
3. A	9. B
4. D	10. D
5. B	11. A
6. B	12. C

Part Two

13. A (children)	17. A (people)
14. C (not)	18. A (Who is)
15. A (What is)	19. B (are)
16. D (across from)	20. C (next to)

UNITS 7–8

Part One

1. D	7. B
2. A	8. D
3. B	9. B
4. D	10. C
5. A	11. B
6. C	12. C

Part Two

13. B (were)	17. B (was)
14. A (Were)	18. B (weren't)
15. B (was)	19. C (were)
16. C (wasn't)	20. B (were you)

UNITS 9–13

Part One

1. B	7. D
2. C	8. B
3. D	9. D
4. A	10. C
5. B	11. A
6. C	12. B

Part Two

13. B (is never)	17. C (has)
14. B (like)	18. C (wakes)
15. B (need)	19. C (cost)
16. B (are always)	20. B (need)

UNITS 14–16

Part One

1. C	7. B
2. C	8. D
3. B	9. B
4. A	10. D
5. A	11. B
6. A	12. C

Part Two

13. B (isn't)	17. B (is)
14. B (are you)	18. B (are growing)
15. C (having)	19. C (practicing)
16. B (going)	20. C (listening)

UNITS 17–20

Part One

1. B	7. D
2. D	8. C
3. C	9. D
4. B	10. B
5. D	11. A
6. C	12. B

Part Two

13. B (can I)
14. A (Cereal)
15. A (This OR That OR The)
16. C (jackets)
17. C (a)
18. B (these)
19. C (meat and rice)
20. C (read)

UNITS 21–23

Part One

1. C	7. D
2. B	8. B
3. D	9. A
4. A	10. D
5. B	11. C
6. D	12. D

Part Two

13. B (drank)	17. A (Who)
14. B (happened)	18. C (did not stay)
15. C (listen)	19. B (have)
16. B (was born)	20. D (say)

UNITS 24–26

Part One

1. B	7. C
2. A	8. D
3. B	9. D
4. B	10. A
5. D	11. C
6. A	12. B

Part Two

13. A (How much)	17. B (a)
14. A (There are)	18. C (they)
15. C (him)	19. A (How many)
16. C (does it)	20. A (Is there)

UNITS 27–30

Part One

1. D	7. B
2. B	8. C
3. C	9. A
4. D	10. C
5. B	11. B
6. D	12. C

Part Two

13. B (the most interesting)
14. C (more interesting)
15. C (on)
16. B (the coldest day)
17. C (a new winter)
18. C (at)
19. C (easier to learn)
20. C (an)

UNITS 31–33

Part One

1. C	7. C
2. D	8. B
3. A	9. C
4. B	10. A
5. D	11. B
6. C	12. C

Part Two

13. B (are you going)
14. A (It's not)
15. A (Am I)
16. B (is he)
17. B (going to be)
18. A (Are Jerry)
19. A (Is)
20. A (Who is going)